ARCANA

ANNA MARIA MORSUCCI • ANTONELLA ALOI

Tarot of MARSEILLE

GUIDE TO INTERPRETATION

LO SCARABEO

Anna Maria Morsucci
Antonella Aloi

TAROT OF MARSEILLE
Guide to Interpretation

Graphics and layout: Chiara Demagistris
Editing: Paolo Bertazzo, Elena Delmastro, Lunaea Weatherstone
Translation: Elizabeth O'Neill, Jessica Noach

Images: Marseille Tarot by Anna Maria Morsucci e Mattia Ottolini

First Edition: Reading and Understanding the Marseille Tarot – © 2018 – Lo Scarabeo
Second Edition: © 2023 – Lo Scarabeo

Printed by Grafiche Stella

Facebook and Instagram: loscarabeotarot

TABLE OF CONTENTS

FOREWORD

The key to this second edition – perhaps the key to the Tarot of Marseille itself – lies in the constant tension between tradition and progress. In its most dialectical form, this tension is exacerbated and becomes a conflict. When this happens, every step forward seems an unforgivable tearing away from tradition and, conversely, every attempt to keep tradition alive appears to be a halt, a burden on evolution and on the need to bring the Tarot's theme in sync with the demands of contemporary life.

On the other hand, when one manages, by luck and will, to break free from this sharp opposition, a different reality emerges, one where tradition and modernity are able to bind together in an interchange of forces and speak to the consultant with a single voice. In this fortunate connection, tradition defines the "what" – in this case, the symbolic wisdom of the Marseille Tarot – and modernity suggests the "how," that is, the way in which the Tarot communicates and interacts with our everyday lives – not in 18th-century Marseille, but here and now.

The main difference between the first and second edition of this volume can be found in the images used as references. The reader will know that, when we speak of the Marseille Tarot, we are not referring to a specific deck, but rather to an iconographic model that developed over more than two centuries, beginning in the late 17th century throughout southern Europe. The first edition of the volume was illustrated with a deck originally printed by Claude Burdel, in Schaffhausen (present-day Switzerland), in 1751.

Working on the first draft of this volume, Anna Maria Morsucci began a systematic and in-depth research of Marseille Tarot's iconography, seeking to isolate its common features, as well as to identify its differences. For Anna

Maria, the creation of a new Marseille deck could only start from a careful research of the foundations laid by tradition. So, a few years later, with the pencils of Mattia Ottolini and the artistic supervision of Pietro Alligo, this new deck was born. Morsucci uses Nicolas Conver's decks from the second half of the 18th century as the original template, supplementing that base with elements and details from older or better-preserved decks. It is a painstaking work of research and historical reconstruction that flows into the contemporary, emerging strengthened by constant comparison with the originals of the time.

The end result gives new life to that unique and inspired combination of tradition and progress, which explains why the Tarot Marseille is still so widespread and beloved. The illustrations in this new deck enrich the volume which you now have in your hands.

Riccardo Minetti

PRESENTATION

For what reason have a coach and a counsellor decided to write a book about the Marseille Tarot? The answer is simple and can be found by going into any bookshop. Looking at the shelves, books can be found that interpret the history and the iconography of the Tarot. Some of these are self-referential, others more subtle. Some books are aimed at a restricted group of initiates, others are exclusively predictive, where questions concerning love, work and money seem to find their answers in the same card. And for those who wish only to know the Tarot, or to gain further insight?

We are talking about the most narrative tool that man has ever invented: learning how to use the Tarot in all its multiplicity, not only as an esoteric or artistic divinatory tool but also one of knowledge and understanding, could be an interesting adventure.

This volume is aimed at those readers who look at the Tarot without preconceived ideas. They are curious and approach it as one would an apparently innocuous game but one rich in suggestion and depth.

As for the two of us, the Tarot has always been a part of our world. Initially we began to be interested in these images as we were curious about a tool that was able to reveal the future. With time, with study and with practice, we realized that these enigmatic figures, full of history, connected to a world populated by kings, queens, emperors and hermits, jesters and angels, speak to us through a symbolic universal language.

The aim of this book is to provide the fundamental tools to build a bridge between intuition and self-reflection. In this way the cards of the Marseille Tarot can be transformed into precious and entertaining life companions, capable of answering simple questions or giving shape to our perceptions. Writing this book was a journey amongst traditional knowledge and suggestions as told by the images. A journey that required attention in order to avoid an excess of cultural references – which would have rendered the text a cold collection of notions – and an excess of fantasies and projections, useful only to us personally.

The cards guided us, Arcanum after Arcanum, toward a road that enabled us to understand the symbols and at the same to listen to our intuitions. How did this occur? Initially we read and studied the most important recognized texts around the subject. Then we analyzed each individual card in all of its complexity and detail, comparing the traditional symbology with suggestions that came to us from the images. And now that this journey has concluded, here is the text. Here experience has come to life, is a spread of words that tell the story of a universe of symbols to be discovered and of epochs to be traversed with the Marseille Tarot.

Anna Maria Morsucci e *Antonella Aloi*

INTRODUCTION

When were Tarot cards born? What do their symbols mean? How do you read them? Is it true they predict the future? Can anyone use them? Do you need a particular predisposition? How can the Tarot figures help us gain greater knowledge?

In this book we will provide the tools for reading and interpreting the Marseille Tarot as well as replying to the former questions and many others. Among the different decks in circulation, we chose the Marseille precisely because they are the messengers of an ancient tradition that hold within them potent universal symbolic values. They are also ones that more than other decks enable us to develop our intuitions and imaginations.

Before beginning however, it is important to clear up one preconception: there is no particular skill required in order to use the cards. Pure and simple curiosity and the capacity to be surprised is the best attitude to have to discover the Tarot. Shall we begin?

CHAPTER ONE

WHAT IS THE TAROT?

Playing cards, sacred texts, a divinatory book, an anthology of popular medieval images, a road to spiritual illumination: these are the Tarot. They are a collection of symbolic suggestions that can be destined for many diverse uses.

The Tarot is a deck of **78 cards** that can describe every aspect of human existence. Like the interweaving of a mosaic, each single card has its own value and meaning and is connected to the others to constitute a unique universe that comprises all of them. In the 78 cards we see first of all two major groups, called the Major Arcana and the Minor Arcana (in Latin *arcanum* means secret).

The Major Arcana are composed of **22 cards** made up of images numbered from 1 to 21 plus one without a number, the Fool, that some experts place at the beginning of the sequence and others at the end.

The Minor Arcana consist of **56 cards** divided into four suits: **Wands, Swords, Cups** and **Pentacles**. These cards are very similar to those that are used for playing Briscola or Tresette (Italian card games), however, while these decks have only 40 cards (10 for each suit from the Ace to 7 plus Page, Horse and King), in the Tarot deck each suit has a sequence of 14 cards that go from the Ace to Ten, called **numerical cards** to which are added the four **Court Figures**: the **Page**, the **Knight**, the **Queen** and the **King**.

WHAT ARE THEY FOR?

A Tarot deck is a book of images where the interpretation is connected to a precise narrative and symbolic code that has passed through the centuries. Contained within it is a variegated universe of knowledge that passes through alchemy, astrology, the Christian religion, Paganism, the ancient philosophies and current esotericisms that renew them from Pythagoras to Plato.

In most cases a deck of Tarot is used above all as a divinatory tool. In actual fact it can have great value even for those who are not interested in peeking into the future. The strength of the Tarot images allows us to enquire into the present and to transform the future into an informed choice. Leafing through the cards signifies entering into contact with a repertoire of people, situations and states of mind. The images are like magnets and activate our intuitions and bring with them other images that help us to see things in more depth and greater lucidity. The Tarot can also be used for meditation and introspection, assisting a dialogue with ourselves and in conversation with others. Professions that assist people, such as psychotherapy, coaching and counseling, can make use of the Arcana to help people to be clear about their desires, convictions and relationships.

For this reason, we have inserted some questions in the descriptions of the Major Arcana and the court figures of the Minor Arcana that are aimed at developing the capacity to imagine and therefore construct personal visons, pathways and objectives. Therefore, the intuitions of each person can be added to the classical meanings of the cards. From our experience this practice has shown itself to be very useful, also for internalizing the meaning of each single card, making it your own, and in this way entering into harmony with the deck.

TAROT AND DIVINATION

How many times have we seen people on the streets who offer to read our futures in the Tarot? This is the most common way in which the cards are used and also the reason why Tarot cards are often associated with charlatans, who profit from the needs or the fears of other people. However, even if the Tarot are used by charlatans, it can be said that "the Tarot is not a charlatan." Like any other tool, it depends on how it is used. Nevertheless, those of us who have chosen to belong to the helping profession do not like and are not interested in thinking that our future is already written. On the contrary, we think this could be dangerous and could constitute an obstacle in terms of personal development if people delegate their destiny to a tool. If, for example, someone asks, "Will I find a job?" and the answer is no, the person could sabotage themselves, close off certain doors and not place themselves in the right frame of mind to realize their own objectives. The use of the Tarot as only a divinatory instrument, useful for negative predictions, risks creating dependency and can determine the future in a sort of "self-fulfilling prophecy". This was described by the sociologist Robert King Merton, according to which a supposition can become a prophecy. The fact itself of just being pronounced makes the event become possible. This is a concept we see on a daily basis in terms of the economy. Market trends are a direct consequence of the expectations regarding a product. Involuntary attitudes such as pessimism, which causes a feeling of distrust, can aggravate an already difficult reality. Our experience has taught us that it is very useful to read the Tarot to analyze the present and to identify possible future scenarios, beginning with the idea that nothing has already been determined. When we do a reading of the cards, we are called to reevaluate the past, to understand the present and to project into the future. If the hypothesized scenario is not to our liking, we need to actuate strategies to change it: doing the exact same things while expecting different results is the height of illusion. Having said this, those who frequently use the Tarot have seen that there is an analogy between the cards that appear and the situation being lived. The fact that a certain card appears could be the result of a phenomena called **synchronicity**, described by the Swiss psychiatrist Carl

Gustav Jung (1875–1961), which explains some phenomena regarding the psychic sphere, such as telepathy for example. According to this intuition, two events can be correlated between themselves by the fact that they can be verified at the same time and are connected by an evident symbolic link. It has probably happened to everyone to have thought of a person and then to bump into them a short time later and perhaps even, that same evening, to see a film where the protagonist has the same name. Similar events happened to Jung in such an evident way as to bring him to formulate this hypothesis. The phenomenon of synchronicity can be associated very easily with the Tarot, or rather to the motivations that bring those who request a consultation to choose one card rather than another. It can therefore be hypothesized that certain cards appear because there is a connection between the event that is being enquired into and the card itself, even if this is not explainable by a cause and effect principle. In this way, what appears as a simple series of coincidences can be interpreted as a sign. In summary, rather than waiting for the card to predict the future, we can choose to listen to the suggestions that they offer and interpret the "coincidences" that can be verified. The Tarot cards, as fascinating as they are, are only a part of a very rich network of symbols. It is up to us to learn how to make sense of them.

CURIOSITY: Carl Gustav Jung, talking about the Tarot, said: "These are psychological images, symbols you can play with, just as the subconscious seems to play with its contents...they combine in certain ways, and the different combinations correspond to the playful development of certain events in the story of humanity....and therefore [the game of Tarot] is adapted to an intuitive method that aims to understand the flow of life, perhaps also to predict future events, events that present themselves to the reading of the conditions of the present moment…"

TAROT AS ARCHETYPES

Carl Gustav Jung, the father of analytic psychology, formulated the theory of the collective subconscious, according to which the functioning of the subconscious in an individual – along with mental activities not consciously present – are based on universal models (archetypes) that are common to all humanity all over the world, regardless of culture and language. This intuition of his, which opened up a path for using Tarot as a tool for introspection and meditation, came from the idea that the Arcana, especially the 22 Major Arcana, contain within them the symbolic representation of reality. Some of the Major Arcana have a direct correspondence with the archetypes defined by Jung. For example, the Magician represents the archetype with the same name, and the Pope that of the "Sage."

The Magician —> Magician

The Hierophant —> Sage

A BIT OF HISTORY

The origin of Tarot cards, of which the most ancient testimonies are Italian, are lost in legend, but we can consider them a fusion of two independent phenomena: **playing cards** and **trump cards.** At the end of the 14th century, a deck of 52 cards divided into four suits, known as the Mamelucco deck (or Cards of Mamelucco), made their way from Egypt through Syria and into Europe. From this deck came the playing cards that we all know and that were spread throughout the continent.

The Major Arcana, known also as the Trumps, can be traced back to a very ancient tradition. The images and symbols of the Trumps belong to a figurative repertoire common in the West, found in the frescoes of the cathedrals and public buildings, in encyclopedic and astrological texts and in the codex of the illuminated manuscripts. Basically, the Trumps were a *Biblia pauperum*, a poor person's Bible, with an educational-recreational objective. Through the images, mystic Christian knowledge and its meaning were diffused.

CURIOSITY: In the Renaissance, from the taverns to the princely courts, Tarot was spread with one aim: that of having fun. In the taverns small fortunes passed from soldiers of fortune to farmers who were very good at the game, in play-offs of games and bets. In the courts, the Tarot were used for games of actual role-playing of a precise literary nature. The "actors" (the members of the court) were assigned the cards extracted from the deck and had to interpret the card as best they could, perhaps reciting a sonnet off the cuff. The participants, all together or one at a time, contributed to the construction of a story.

The figures present on the Major Arcana, therefore, have not derived from a void and are influenced by preexisting images. To illustrate this close relationship and interchange, a look at a few images will be enough.

The high relief in terracotta known as the *Burney Relief*, dating from the 19th to 18th century BCE, represents the winged goddess Inanna, with paws and eagle talons. This can be compared to Arcanum XV, the Devil, both for the posture and for its attributes.

Inanna
(Burney Relief)

The Devil
(Arcanum XV)

The images on the tombstone of Alexander the Great exactly reproduces the posture and the scene that is represented in Arcanum VII, the Chariot.

The flight of Alexander
(Stone slab, XII sec.)

The Chariot
(Arcanum VII)

This influence can also be noted in a work by the Dutch painter known to the public under his pseudonym of **Hieronymus Bosch** (1453–1516). In this painting a very common scene on the streets at that time is depicted: an illusionist, just like the Arcanum I, the Magician.

"The Conjurer"
by Hieronymus Bosch

The Magician
(Arcanum I)

Finally, one of the abstract masterpieces by **Pablo Picasso** (1881–1973), where, unconsciously or not, the artist depicts a seated woman and uses the exact same emphasis on color and the same posture as the Arcanum III – the Empress.

"Femme au chapeau jaune et vert"
by Pablo Picasso

The Empress
(Arcanum III)

These examples confirm that the aesthetic and the structure of the Tarot of Marseille, which at first glance can seem to be simple and even rudimentary, bring with them an evocative force that crosses over time, fashion and historical contexts.

THE "PHILOSOPHY" OF THE TAROT

The years when the first Tarot decks made their appearance in the Italian courts were characterized by the recovery of classical Latin and Greek texts. In this exact period, the philosopher, humanist and priest **Marsilio Ficino** (1433–1499) translated the *Corpus Hermeticum,* a collection of writings that played a fundamental role in Western esoteric traditions. It was important in the development of doctrines of a secret or initiatory nature that had as their objective the revelation of occult truths to their adepts. Attributed to the legendary personality **Hermes Trismegistus**, under whose name (which means "Hermes the Thrice-Greatest"), a vast literature in Greek was developed. Dating from the first to the second century CE, the writings of *Corpus Hermeticum* concern the so-called occult sciences, which were astrology and alchemy, as well as the secret virtues of plants and stones. When the Italian humanists gained possession of these writings they were greatly influenced. This knowledge is contained in a Tarot deck: the analogies; the cryptic or manifest symbols that can be observed in nature are represented in a stylized and evocative manner in the cards, transforming the entire deck into a complex and beautiful unique item.

NOTES: The phrase "what is above is like that which is below", attributed to Hermes Trismegistus, is taken from the Emerald Tablet, which was published in Arabic between the 6th and the 8th centuries and spread to the Christian West up until the 14th century. It reflects the complex scheme upon which the structure of the cards of the Tarot were structured.

Thus Italy gave the world the Tarot – the cards and the game – and France the occult and their use for divination.

FROM ITALY TO FRANCE

A game played in taverns, a lyrical entertainment for the privileged classes in the Italian courts, an initiation tool for the selected few: for these reasons Tarot was born and developed in Italy. The divinatory use of the cards became very popular only at the end of the 18th century. It was a Frenchman, **Antoine Court de Gébelin**, who considered the Tarot strictly in esoteric and divinatory terms. He was an archaeologist and a mason. In 1781 he wrote an article, published in the monumental and unfinished encyclopedia *Mondo Primitivo,* indicating that the Tarot was a residual of the *Book of Thoth*, a legendary prophetic text attributed to the Egyptian god of magic, a precursor of the Greek god Hermes and inventor of hieroglyphics. The relationship between Tarot and the divinatory arts became evident in his hypothesis, actually made without any scientific basis at all. The ideas of Gebélin were analyzed and further investigated by a number of occultists. The foremost of these was a contemporary, **Jean-Baptiste Alliette**, better known by his pseudonym of **Etteilla,** who came to the conclusion that the Tarot had lost its original characteristics over the course of the centuries. He therefore decided to produce a deck that would give back, what according to him, was their original primitive form. Etteilla came to declare that these cards hid the secrets of universal medicine and that they could be used to predict the future. Successively, in 1855, the esoterist and occultist **Eliphas Lévi** elaborated a theory based on the fact that the Major Arcana were 22 cards, the same number as the letters of the Hebrew alphabet. This suggested to Lévi that there was perhaps a connection between the Tarot and the Kabbalah.

NOTES: The system of the Kabbalah is articulated in the so-called Tree of Life. For Kabbalists it represents all of the manifestations of God, where the process of creation is symbolized by the ten sephiroths, or spheres, and the 22 paths that unite them. If one follows this map, and connects the Tarot with the Kabbalah, each Major Arcanum can correspond to one of these paths, and vice versa, each path is associated with an Arcanum. Furthermore, in the Kabbalist numerology, 22 symbolizes a magic number that represents the sum of knowledge applied to problems of a practical nature.

Gerard Encausse (1865–1916), a noted person in the Kabbalist Order of the Rosicrucians, known under the name of **Papus**, created a deck of Tarot where the protagonists were presented in Egyptian dress. He was inspired by Tarots diffused in Bohemia and attributed them with an initiatory value.

Oswald Wirth (1860–1943), a Swiss esoterist, astrologer and writer, dedicated himself intensely to studying the Tarot and created his own deck which goes back to the Marseille Tarot. He however inserted a series of symbols and meanings that guide modern students of esotericism still today.

NOTES: Oswald Wirth had the ability to perceive and synthesize the most important current esoteric thinking and principles of his time. He was aware of the universal value of the symbols, united the teachings of diverse esoteric schools and enabled them to come together in a common matrix. Based on the Marseille Tarot, he redesigned the 22 Major Arcana and tried, as much as possible, to recover the ancient symbolic aspects, as well as the colors and the esoteric meanings.

THE MARSEILLE TAROT

The Tarot was born in Italy and spread to France thanks to the exchanges between the two countries, which has been well documented by historians. Why Marseille exactly? It was the French city where this type of card was produced. As a production center, Marseille became active much later than other centers such as Rouen or Lyon, and received the Royal License for production only in 1631. It rapidly became the major center of the country however. The oldest deck that can be classified as Marseillaise with certainty was designed around 1650 by the card manufacturer **Jean Noblet**. Nevertheless, there are older decks, from 1499, that contain elements similar to the Marseille. It was in 1499 that France invaded and annexed Milan, creating the opportunity (via the French soldiers) for the Tarot to be spread from Italy to France, bringing with them the graphic elements that were later developed in the Marseille model. The city of Marseille as an important port city facilitated the diffusion of the French Tarot throughout Europe, and amongst the variety of types that flourished at this time, the Marseille became the most important.

NOTES: The great card producers often came from a dynasty of printers who passed down the secrets of their art from one generation to the next. Putting aside the name of the Arcanum at the bottom of each figure, often written in an unusual French that has been a source of much speculation among esoterists, an indication of the printer and the year of production can be found on the Two of Pentacles or the Two of Cups. In this way it was possible to discover hundreds of manufacturers who were active between the 1700s and the 1800s, most of them deployed above all in the southeastern regions of France, from Switzerland, Belgium and northern Italy. Among the more active families in the production of the Marseille were the Arnoux (Marseille, 1790–1829), Benoit (Strasburg, 1751–1803), Conver (Marseille, 1760–1950), Fautrier (Marseille, 1753–1793), Grimaud (Paris, 1748–1950), Madenié (Dijon, around 1700–1795), and Tourcaty (Marseille, 1701–1809). Other families were in Switzerland: Burdel (Freiburg, 1751–1850), Rochias (Neuchatel, around 1775–1850) and Schaer (Mümliswil, around 1730–1896).

The commercial success of the Marseille Tarot, which allowed for the extraordinary diffusion of these cards, was not only due to the economic strength of the French in the 1700s but also to the advanced artisan techniques which were the best of that era. This enabled them to produce a greater number of decks, of better quality with respect to their competitors, and at a lower cost.

CURIOSITY: The procedure for the printing of a deck of Marseille Tarot began with the work of an incisor, who designed and cut out the figures on a large piece of dried wood or a copper sheet. With this matrix the outlines of the figures were printed, only in black. Then, once the sheets were dry, a perforated screen was placed over these and the first color was painted by hand. Once that was dry, another color was applied with the relative screen. Finally, the sheets were cut and the cards put together to form a deck, which was then covered in a special wrapping. During the same period, the Italians, considered at the time to be the best printers of cards, used a much longer and more expensive procedure: each card was glued onto a sheet, the edges of which were turned around the figure in order to reinforce the borders.

The title "Marseille Tarot" was not introduced prior to 1930, when the Grimaud company, on the initiative of its director, **Paul Marteau**, produced a re-edition of the model, which at that time was simply called "Italian Tarot." The deck of Marseille Tarot realized by Grimaud can be considered as a new version of the Conver deck of 1760. Paul Marteau called the deck the "Ancient Tarot of Marseille." The Grimaud edition proved to be very popular and is still in print today. In 1948 Marteau wrote and published a book, *The Tarot of Marseille*, which revolutionized the interpretation of the numerical cards of the Minor Arcana.

Many years later, in 1997, the Chilean artist **Alejandro Jodorowsky** and the descendent of the master card producers Conver, **Philippe Camoin**, produced a new restoration of the Marseille Tarot. It is characterized by a reinterpretation of the forms and the colors, to which have been added numerous variations.

THE MARSEILLE CANON

Why would anyone today be interested in the Marseille Tarot that has such ancient workmanship? Their images can seem mediocre if compared to the technical skill and to the more explicit symbolism of other decks. Often there are only four colors; at times the faces of the figures are almost grotesque. Furthermore, the suit cards (from the Ace to the Ten), are similar to playing cards, which differ from modern Tarot decks. So why the Marseille? Because they have a quality that cannot be found in the other types of Tarot. To begin with, the fact that the deck does not follow any modern aesthetic standard renders the images timeless, releasing them from our cultural and social expectations. The illustrations appear simple and without explicit reference to esoteric systems such as the Kabbalah, astrology or alchemy, which can be found in other decks. Another aspect to keep in mind is that the creators of the Marseille did not leave any instruction booklet, leaving the liberty of interpreting the cards up to the users. For this reason, the suggestions for interpretation that can be found in this book are exactly that: simple suggestions, even if they do take into account the numerological and symbolic aspects that were certainly known at the time in which the Marseille Tarot was developed. Objectively one Tarot deck is not "better" than another, but the intention of this book is to aid in the comprehension of the Marseille Tarot, in their extraordinary uniqueness.

CHAPTER TWO

THE STRUCTURE OF THE TAROT DECK

The Marseille Tarot, as previously stated, is composed of 78 cards, subdivided into **22 Major Arcana** and **56 Minor Arcana**. Before looking at the details, a brief overview of the logic used in the structuring of the deck will be given.

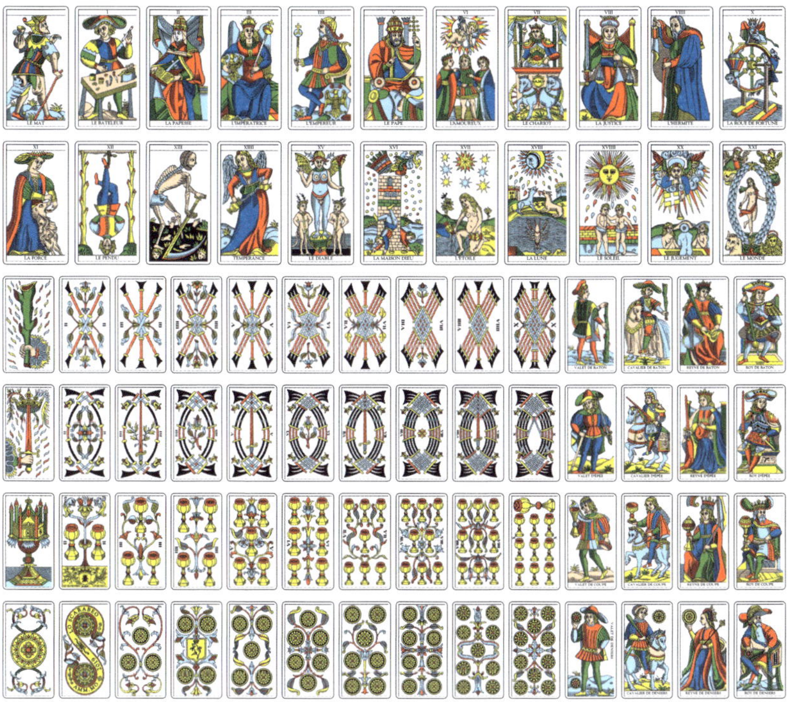

THE MAJOR ARCANA

The 22 cards that compose the Major Arcana describe an initiation path that starts with the Creation and through various stages arrives at perfection. The images on the cards represent the principal events of life and their origins, their strong points, the road to follow, the dangers that are best avoided, and provide important indications of a general nature.

The sequence of the Major Arcana is as follows:

0 – The Fool

I – The Magician

II – The High Priestess

III – The Empress

IIII – The Emperor

V – The Hierophant

VI – The Lovers

VII – The Chariot

VIII – Justice

VIIII – The Hermit

X – The Wheel of Fortune

XI – Strength

XII – The Hanged Man

XIII – (unnamed Arcanum)

XIIII – Temperance

XV – The Devil

XVI – The Tower

XVII – The Star

XVIII – The Moon

XVIIII – The Sun

XX – Judgment

XXI – The World

The Fool, which doesn't have a number, can be placed at the beginning, as was done here, or at the end of the Major Arcana sequence.

THE MINOR ARCANA

The 56 Minor Arcana are often ignored and considered secondary and for many are difficult to interpret, but they represent a guide for inquiry into the practical aspects of life. They provide indications about the details that define a situation. The Minor Arcana are divided into four suits: **Wands, Swords, Cups** and **Pentacles.** Each suit is composed of 10 numerical cards that range from **One** to **Ten**, plus four court figures: the **Page**, the **Knight**, the **Queen** and the **King**.

CURIOSITY: Each suit could represent a sphere of our existence, and an analogy could be made with one of the four elements that according to the ancient philosophers, composed reality: Fire (energy), Air (thought), Water (emotion), Earth (matter). Each suit, in fact, refers to the characteristics of the element. The Wands could be lit by fire; the Swords glide through air; Cups contain liquid; Pentacles are the metals that can be found in the earth.

THE FOUR SUITS

What do the four suits represent therefore? Certain experts maintain that they could symbolize the social classes that were present in Europe in the Middle Ages. According to this theory, the Wands would represent the manual workers of the fields and forests such as peasants and laborers; the Swords the nobility; the Cups the clerics; and the Pentacles the merchants.

The following is a brief overview of the meaning of the suits, which will be explained in greater detail in the following pages:

The **cards of Wands** represent energy, creativity, enthusiasm, growth, progress, ambition and strength. They also indicate manual activity.

The **cards of Swords** are connected to mental and spiritual development, to intellectual capacity, courage and obstacles to be overcome. They indicate intellectual activity.

The **cards of Cups** are connected to female aspects, to receptiveness, passivity, the uterus, the breasts. The image of a vase represents the efficient functions of a mother, in other words, to contain and maintain life (water), to protect and nourish (food).

The **cards of Pentacles** are connected to material and financial security, practical resources, the physical body, work, friendship, and family stability. As with metals that can be found in the earth, they express the concreteness of matter.

NUMBERS, MYSTERIOUS NUMBERS!

Looking at the 78 cards all together, it can be seen that they are all connected by constant references that are apparent throughout the deck.

Here is an example:

The hat of the Magician (Arcanum I) refers to that of Strength (Arcanum XI)

In the Magician (Arcanum I) the four suits (which refer to the four elements) are the objects placed upon the table and can be identified with the four figures on the corners of the card the World (Arcanum XXI).

These references, which will be mentioned often and which you are invited to discover by looking at the cards, follow numerological criteria. When we talk about numbers, our minds go straight to the mathematics that were taught at school with formulas and complex expressions. In the case of the Marseille Tarot, entering into harmony with the numbers is the most fundamental way to understand their meaning. There is nothing to be afraid of: this knowledge is part of the Western symbolic system in which all of us, even unconsciously, are immersed. Let's look at why.

Our history begins with the Greek philosopher **Pythagoras** (570–495 BCE) – whose theory of the triangle we all studied at school – who used numbers in order to explain reality and the universe. As a young man he was also a student of the occult sciences. Arriving in Egypt, he was initiated into the mysteries of the priests in the land of the Pharaohs. Following this, he founded a school of mystic philosophy where he maintained that numbers are the principle of all things, that the universe is a harmonious entity (a cosmos), that the celestial bodies, with their movement, gave origin to sound (the music of the spheres), that the soul is immortal and passes through numerous bodies (metempsychosis), and that the final stage of man is his beatitude and his reaching a divine status. All of this is very fascinating, but what does it have to do with Tarot? And above all, what does it have to do with us?

For Pythagoras, the entire universe was contained in the **first four numbers**, which expressed the foundation of all things that together generated the **Ten (1+2+3+4=10)**, and which is considered the visible manifestation of Everything. He called Ten the "root of eternal Nature." The structure of the Tarot deck takes into account this vision, following the main esoteric currents that were present during the Renaissance, in particular that of Hermeticism – referring to the mystic figure of Hermes Trismegistus, who was previously discussed. Apart from the practical and exclusively mathematical meaning, therefore, it also has a symbolic and philosophical value.

Let us briefly consider the meaning of the first four numbers according to Pythagoras.

One identifies the point, without dimensions or any kind of principle.

Two builds a straight line, the union between two points, therefore possessing only one dimension: length

Three, the union of three points, forms a triangle and is the consequence of one level, that has length and width but not thickness.

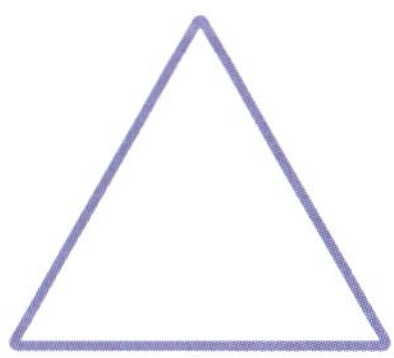

An equilateral triangle, where each point is connected to the other two points, has three equal sides and contains three equal angles. This geometric figure is the base of sacred geometry for the mystics inspired by Pythagoras. In alchemy, however, it is the representation of nature, and in fact the symbols of the four elements are all based on the triangle.

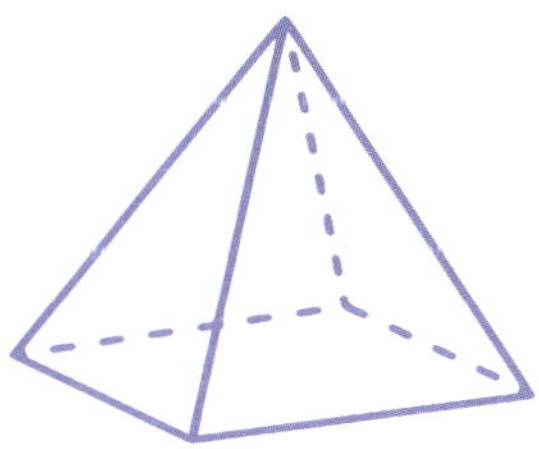

Four represents the manifestation of the solid figure. By adding one point to the previous three, the most simple solid geometric shape is obtained: a tetrahedron, the pyramid with a square base, with three dimensions. It

is not a coincidence that the Egyptians constructed the pyramids with this shape. This number therefore is the expression of divine perfection. An example of this aspect of 4 comes from the biblical tetragram, the name of God expressed by the four letters YHWH.

The numbers 1, 2, 3, and 4 are the origin of the Tetrad (*Tetràktys*), the design of mathematical sequence that the Pythagoreans venerated to the point of swearing allegiance to him. Observing the Tetrad, it can be seen that each line is attained by adding a unit to the following line. 1+1=2, 2+1=3 and so on.

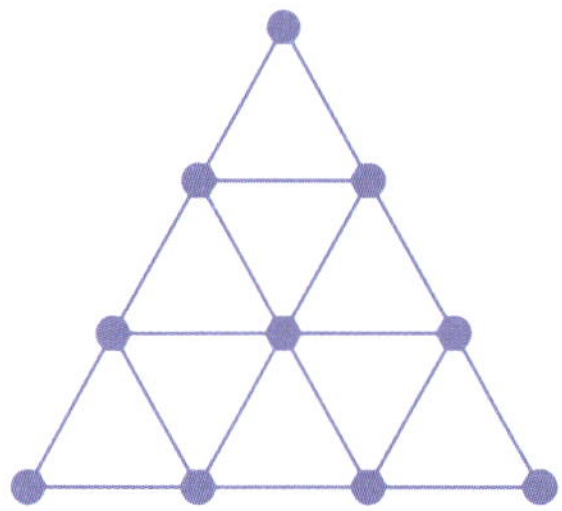

NOTES: The number 4 is connected to the geometric form of the square. If the square is united with the triangle – by placing the upper side of the square with the base of the triangle – a new geometric shape is obtained, called septenary as it is connected to the number 7, the sum of 3 and 4 (3+4=7). This is one of the key elements for subdividing the Arcana.

To complete this section, a brief analysis of the predecessors of Tarot is provided: **dice**. Tarot cards have a very similar structure to dice used for playing, and probably come from them. The first six Major Arcana are matched among themselves in an exactly analogous way as the six sides of a dice: **the sum total of each of the opposite sides of a dice is always equal to 7.**

This analogy allows us to introduce another numerological argument connected to Tarot: the division by sevens. The number 7 – as will be seen shortly – is very important and is present in numerous manifestations of our lives since ancient times: there are seven planets in the solar system visible to the naked eye; seven days in a week; seven mortal sins described in the Bible.

THE SUBDIVISION BY SEVENS

The sequence of the Major Arcana, excluding the Fool, can be divided into three groups of seven cards, that seem to describe the passages of human life.

The first seven Arcana (from the Magician to the Chariot) represent the physical world and correspond to that period of life in which a person becomes aware of their own individual abilities and their own actions. **The second seven** (from Justice to Temperance) symbolize the world of ideas. The tension of the individual in his/her search for his/her own place in the world. **The third set of seven** (from the Devil to the World) indicate a divine path. In other words, this is an inner journey of evolving knowledge until one reaches full satisfaction, through the ability to reconcile the material and the spiritual aspects of existence.

In the first seven Arcana the terrestrial journey of the Fool occurs, or rather, our journey: we meet people who have a role in society, which is connected to a symbolic value. Furthermore, we confront situations from which we can learn something. Becoming the Magician, we must measure up to reality, acquiring the qualities of the High Priestess, the Empress, the Emperor, and the Hierophant. We must make choices (the Lovers) and start new journeys (the Chariot).

In the second sequence, we must learn a series of virtues and qualities: Justice, Temperance, Strength. To become wise (the Hermit), testing ourselves with alternate episodes of destiny (the Wheel of Fortune), look at things from another point of view (the Hanged Man), and to know how to change, leaving behind what we no longer need (Arcanum without a name – Death).

Finally, in the third sequence, we learn to feel part of a universe that is much greater than us. We face our dark sides, our fears and our ego (the Devil), putting our ambitions into perspective and defeating pride, freeing us from conditioning (the Tower) and entering into contact with the elements of the Cosmos (the Star, the Moon, the Sun). A new life is born (Judgment) in order to reach perfection (the World).

This will be our journey.

Once the cycle has terminated, we begin again: perfection is not eternal nor immutable. We have our first map for a journey we are aware that we are about to begin.

NOTES: The journey is a cycle that does not foresee a return: in fact, the sequence of Roman numerals that are found on all of the Arcana are progressive. For example, the four is indicated by the sign IIII (1+1+1+1) not IV (5–1). Also, the language of the images follows the same progressive tendency: our left represents the past, our right the future. We will verify these aspects by analyzing the individual cards.

THE SUBDIVISION IN TENS

In the Major Arcana, other than the division by sevens, we can also find another division, composed of two sets of ten, where the Arcana are grouped according to the last letter of their number. Therefore, the High Priestess (Arcanum II) and the Hanged Man (Arcanum XII) are connected. Two Arcana are the exception – the World (Arcanum XXI) and the Fool (0). The World dominates all of the Arcana and represents the sum of all the other Tarot cards. The Fool, on the contrary, represents the number 0 and is seen as outside of any hierarchy. It is considered separate and complementary to all the other Tarot cards. The subdivision in ten is present also in the numerical cards of the Minor Arcana, which are ten for each suit. The Minor Arcana therefore are connected to the Major Arcana in function of their number. Returning to the Major Arcana, in the first ten, from the Magician to the Wheel of Fortune, we find a series of human or animal figures which can be found in situations and practical activities, all of which are very understandable. The landscape is almost absent and within this the figures and their actions appear dominant. In the second set of ten, from Strength to Justice, there are scenery and situations where the human figure appears to be inserted into a landscape that gradually becomes richer, with references to the forces of nature and the cosmos becoming more evident. Furthermore, following the sequence of the Arcana, the allegorical and fantasy aspects increase. It is very interesting to place the two Major Arcana sets of ten side by side: immediately it can be seen that the images of the cards express the same concepts with the opposite meanings. These are two diverse and opposite paths, but our journey through the Tarot requires us to know and to try both of them.

The Major Arcana divided into tens

THE MEANING OF THE NUMBERS APPLIED TO THE TAROT

In both the Major Arcana and the Minor Arcana, numbers play an important role in understanding the meaning of the cards. The interpretation is in fact connected to the symbolic aspect expressed by the numerical value of the Arcana and the associated geometric forms. For example, all of the fours (including the Arcanum IV and the Arcanum XIV) share certain characteristics typical of the nature of the number 4, such as stability. In the analysis of the number it needs to be kept in mind that traditionally even and uneven numbers are subdivided. The uneven numbers represent the active principle (masculine) while the even numbers represent the receptive principle (feminine).

From all this explanation, one Arcanum is missing, the Fool, which is the number 0: a digit that indicates nothingness, absence and emptiness, but which, placed after another digit, can change the order of magnitude (1 becomes 10, then 100, then 1000 and so on). And so, the Fool can take on any appearance, embodying all the other 21 cards of the Major Arcana.

NOTE: In the case that you have found this section too complex or lacking in validation, we suggest you read it over again after having reviewed all 78 Arcana, which are explained in detail in the following chapters. It will become easier to understand why we thought it important to broach this topic now.

The following is a synthesis of the meanings of the numbers from 1 (I) to 10 (X).

Potential and completeness, the beginning of something or the top of a hierarchy

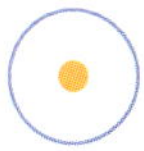

1 is the first of all the numbers. Each number, multiplied or divided by 1 remains the same. Furthermore, each number is divisible by 1. This makes it a measure or a point of reference for all the other existing numbers.

It is associated with the supreme divine and symbolizes the act itself of creation. Furthermore, it is connected to privilege and to importance: it indicates the vertex of every hierarchical order.

In geometry: The number 1 is represented by a point, the simplest geometric form, which does not have a shape or dimension but from which everything begins.

Keywords: Principle, unity, power.

In the Tarot: This card connects with seven Tarot cards: three Major Arcana and four Minor Arcana. In the Magician (Arcanum I) it indicates creative potential. In Strength (Arcanum XI) it brings the component of a new beginning and sanctions the passage toward a more receptive phase, one with greater reference to the intellectual and spiritual world. In the World (Arcanum XXI) it is meant as unity, a form of completeness that concludes the sequence of the Major Arcana. In the Minor Arcana: The Ace (number 1 of the numerical cards) represents potentiality and can be considered as a spark from which the other cards of the same suit are born and are developed. It is also seen as the greatest manifestation and purest of the concepts connected to that suit.

Duplicity: a complementary union but also conflict

The number 2 suggests that something has begun and that the events are already in motion. It represents union or the meeting between two elements, in the same way that two weights can be compared on a scale. The number 2 indicates choice, the need to decide between two possibilities, It also represents fertility, the meeting between two different beings and from which a third is born.

It is the emblem of the couple. It indicates an association but also a contrast between two ways of being, a struggle, a rivalry.

In geometry: The number 2 is represented by a line, intended as the shortest distance between two points.

Keywords: Duality, meeting, collision/confrontation

In the Tarot: The number 2 connects six Tarot cards: two from the Major Arcana and four from each suit. The High Priestess (Arcanum II) expresses the separation and the coexistence of two opposites: the material and the spiritual, the visible and the invisible. In the Hanged Man (Arcanum XII) it indicates a clear opposition between two worlds or two polarities. In the Minor Arcana: The number 2 represents, for each suit, the accumulation of opposite or complementary energies. In this sense it could be considered as an encounter or a confrontation between two equally strong entities.

The "perfect number," the solution of conflicts, balance of opposites, creation

The number 3 represents creation, as the number 1 on its own, even if potentially creative, is in fact barren because, even if multiplied by itself, it is always 1. The number 2 doesn't solve the problem because, when confronted with the number 1, it remains the number 2. To reconcile the opposites and create other numbers, 3 is necessary. It indicates something that leads to fulfillment as a result of overcoming the conflict generated in the number 2, and the creation of something new – a birth. The number has a deep mystic significance: in Christianity, the Trinity is composed of the Father, Son and Holy Ghost.

It represents the solution to a problem or a choice that has brought new consequences. It also indicates mediation between two opposites.

In geometry: The number 3 is represented by an equilateral triangle, which arises from the union of three points.

Keywords: Perfection, construction, birth.

In the Tarot: Six Tarot cards are connected to the number 3: two Major Arcana and the Three of each suit. In the Empress (Arcanum III) it expresses a mother's creativity and thus the mystery of life. In the Unnamed Arcanum (Death – Arcanum XIII) it expresses a complementary concept, that is birth that leads to death, which in turn leads to rebirth. In the Minor Arcana: The Three, in the four suits, embodies the idea of birth as an expansion of energy. It should be interpreted as the moment in which the forces at stake, after having confronted, measured or challenged themselves, establish the birth of a new situation.

Perfection of stability and of order, manifestation of the energies on the material plane

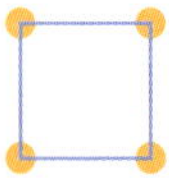

The number 4 represents solidity as four points are needed to build the simplest of geometric solids (the tetrahedron). Furthermore, according to traditional cosmologies, everything in the sensory world is made up of a mixture of four different elements (Fire, Earth, Air and Water) in different proportions and is characterized by a mixture of four essential qualities (Dry, Moist, Cold, Warm). Solid matter is therefore symbolized by the number 4, which also represents the Earth.

It indicates security, order, stasis, and the concreteness of matter.

In geometry: The number 4 is represented by a square, a regular figure that symbolizes the demarcation of space in an orderly way and within well-defined confines.

Keywords: Concreteness, stability, stasis.

In the Tarot: Six Tarot cards are connected to the number 4: two Major Arcana and the Four of each suit. In the Emperor (Arcanum IIII) it expresses the consolidation that comes from the order and stability of the elements, in Temperance (Arcanum XIIII) it harmonizes the temperaments expressed by stability, tempering its excesses with adaptability. In the Minor Arcana: The Four represents the consolidation of the qualities expressed by the four suits and can be considered a balanced base on which to build, or a reference point in the midst of change.

Overcoming stability, imbalance but also mediation between different realities

The number 5 is the sum of 4 + 1 and is characterized by a lack of equilibrium: an element is added and it is necessary to work on the matter to create a new equilibrium. Its dynamic and potentially destructive nature also contains the expression of the will and power of man, which are the basis of magic.

It indicates change, uncertainty, an obstacle that leads to renewal.

In geometry: The number 5 is represented by the pentagon, that symbolically indicates man: the vertices represent the head, legs and arms (like the Vitruvian Man of artist and scientist Leonardo da Vinci 1452–1519). The pentagon can also be depicted as a five-pointed star which, if inscribed in a circle, is called a pentacle.

Keywords: Transformation, revolution, agitation.

In the Tarot: Six Tarot cards are connected to the number 5: two Major Arcana and the Five of each suit. Both in the Hierophant (Arcanum V) and in the Devil (Arcanum XV) the number 5 expresses the influence of man and is perceived as the mediation between matter and the divine. In the Minor Arcana: The Five represents the liberation of the energy expressed by the suit to which it belongs. In this sense, it indicates the restlessness and imperfection of man, who engages in the search for a solution that is often destructive, at least in the short term, but that allows him to overcome his limitations.

Equilibrium, two opposing realities that complement each other

The number 6 is the sum of 3 + 3 (or 4 + 2) and represents union and perfection, as well as the result of the interaction of two perfect entities that attract or repel each other. The two parts that make up the number 6 have the same weight and are balanced between them. Therefore, their equilibrium, while dynamic and sometimes favoring one aspect over the other, leads to complementarity and not to conflict.

It indicates order and perfection and allows us to make sense of what we are and what we wish to be.

In geometry: The number 6 is represented by the hexagon, a regular polygon in which all sides and all angles are equal. The hexagon can fill a plane without leaving empty space: this attribute further enhances the harmony of the geometric figure.

Keywords: Union, comparison, analysis.

In the Tarot: For number 6 there are as many Tarot cards: two Major Arcana and the Six of each suit. In the Lovers (Arcanum VI) it expresses the choice of the individual between two paths, while in the Tower (Arcanum XVI) it represents a choice that concerns the world in its broadest meaning. In the Minor Arcana: Six, within the suit to which it belongs, represents the form that emerges from the chaos, or the equilibrium that is reached after turbulence. In this sense we can interpret the act of choosing as a path that brings order and directs our actions.

Ability to rise and overcome your limits, wisdom

The number 7 is very important due to its mystical value which makes it the symbol of the elevation of man toward the infinite. As the union of 3 + 4 it is the emblem of completion and perfection. It is called the "number of the Spheres" as in the Middle Ages it was thought that the heavens were divided in seven concentric Spheres, each connected to a planet (from the Sun to Saturn), beyond which there were the Zodiacal heavens and finally the Prime Mover (i.e. God).

It represents the need to overcome one's limits and the triumph of spirit over matter.

In geometry: The number 7 is graphically represented by the heptagram, a seven-pointed star. This figure is traditionally used to indicate, for example, the seven planets of astrology or the seven alchemical metals. The star indicates the lack of symmetry that emerges when the human meets the divine and is driven to transcend.

Keywords: Elevation, development, effort.

In the Tarot: Six Tarot cards are connected to the number 7: two Major Arcana and the Seven of each suit. In the Chariot (Arcanum VII) it expresses the ability to elevate oneself and exercise self-control; in the Star (Arcanum XVII) it expresses a different vision of elevation that no longer depends on ambition and the strength of means, but on the knowledge of oneself and the understanding of the world. In the Minor Arcana: Seven, in the context of each suit, expresses the ability to overcome one's limits and transcend matter.

Infinity, harmony and order even where chaos seems to dominate

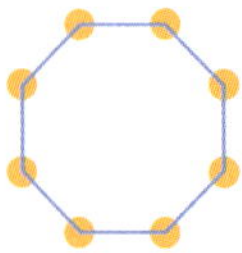

The number 8 can be seen as the sum of 4 + 4, hence its double, and can indicate completeness, understood as the achieving of material fulfillment, and justice, considered as the balance between two different modes that is obtained through constant and periodic change of perspective. The number 8 is called the "number of infinity". In fact, the symbol of infinity is an 8 lying on its side, indicating the continuity of existence.

It represents balance and orderly evolution.

In geometry: The number 8 is geometrically represented by the octagon, a graphic expression of physical and spiritual equilibrium, and of space. It is often found in churches and cathedrals, especially in numerous Christian baptisteries or baptismal fonts.

Keywords: Evolution, natural cycles, completeness.

In the Tarot: Six Tarot cards are connected to the number 8: two Major Arcana and the Eight of each suit. In Justice (Arcanum VIII) it indicates balance and the ability to evaluate before acting; in the Moon (Arcanum XVIII) the lunar phases express an unchanging natural order even if tied to constant change. In the Minor Arcana: The Eight, in the context of the suit to which it belongs, expresses the constant renewal that comes from the search for perfection, and indicates the ability to look in different directions and find unexpected solutions to the obstacles we face.

Maximum growth and the desire to go further

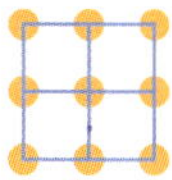

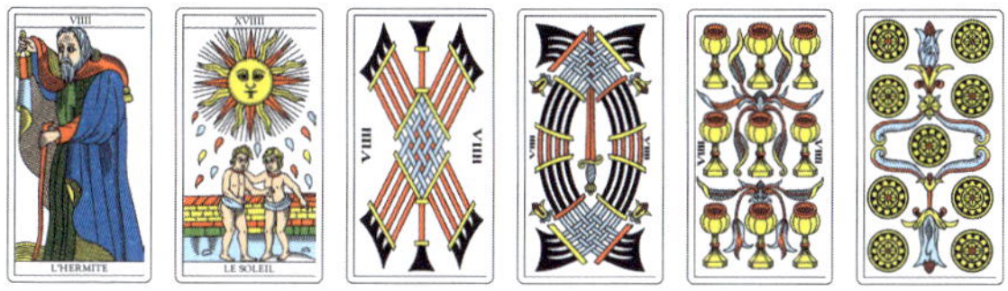

The number 9 is called the "magic number of initiates" because of its great properties. The 9 arises from the multiplication of the perfect number 3 by itself. As the last of the single-digit numbers, it indicates the threshold, the transition from the world of matter to that of the spirit. In Christian tradition there are nine levels of angelic hierarchy, which is why the Divine Comedy of Dante Alighieri is divided into three canticas of 33 cantos each for a total of 99 cantos.

It expresses experience, awareness, the ability to cross the threshold.

In geometry: The number 9 is graphically represented by three rows of three points each, arranged in such a way as to outline a square. The multiplication by three of the number symbolizes the passage between plane and space, between two and three dimensions, and therefore between the square and the cube.

Keywords: Experience, awareness, threshold.

In the Tarot: Six Tarot cards are connected to the number 9: two Major Arcana and the Nine of each suit. In the Hermit (Arcanum VIIII) who illuminates his journey with a lamp, it expresses the search for truth, the solitary meditation; in the Sun (Arcanum XVIIII) which illuminates the world, it indicates a shared knowledge. In the Minor Arcana: The Nine represents, for each suit, something that is about to manifest itself but which must be managed wisely, alluding to omens and new forces taking shape in the world.

The maximum has been reached,
it is time to start again

The number 10 is called the "number of knowledge" for its ability – as we saw when we talked about the tetractys – to contain the Whole (1 +2 +3 +4 = 10). It is therefore the number which contains all and represents the goal and the end of each path.

It represents completeness, the end of a cycle and the beginning of another, to be carried out by bringing along the wisdom from experiences and what has been learned.

In geometry: As we have already seen, the number 10 is represented graphically by the tetractys, a figure which has 10 triangle points on four rows of 4, 3, 2 and 1 point respectively, to which the Pythagoreans attributed a sacred value.

Keywords: Fulfillment, completeness, end of a cycle.

In the Tarot: Six Tarot cards are connected to the number 10: two Major Arcana and the Ten of each suit. In the Wheel of Fortune (Arcanum X) it expresses the continuous, cyclic and eternal flow of life, through which reality lives in perpetual renewal; while Judgment (Arcanum XX) represents the final awakening, the definitive fulfillment of every physical, mental or spiritual transformation. In the Minor Arcana: Ten, in the four suits, represents completeness in different areas.

THE COURT FIGURES

The 16 court figures of the Minor Arcana (four for each suit) are: **Page**, **Knight**, **Queen** and **King**, whose order reflects earthly hierarchies and age (from the youngest and unripe to the most mature and expert). Because of their nature, they do not lend themselves to numerological interpretation. Below is a brief indication of the meaning of the four court figures:

THE PAGES

The initial spark

The Page, also known as the prince, describes a situation or a person in our life. In the first case it is a completely new circumstance or one that has just begun; in the second case, a youth or an unknown aspect of our personality that will find a way to express itself.

THE KNIGHTS

Action, courage, determination

The figure of the Knight is probably linked to the ancient chivalric orders. It can represent a situation or a person about to arrive. In the first case it symbolizes action, movement and progress; if it indicates a person, he/she will be young, adventurous and active.

THE QUEENS

Careful Reflection, listening

The Queen refers to the feminine, in its various meanings. It can represent an important woman in our life, or a significant, clear, and receptive aspect of our personality, both for men and for women.

THE KINGS

Maturity, wisdom, authority

In ancient traditions, the King is associated with the figure of a man of power, fully established in his role. It can indicate male figures of authority who express different character traits, important men, or an aspect of personality that needs to be developed, harnessed or checked.

ARCANA AND SYMBOLS

All 78 Tarot cards are full of symbols that draw inspiration from images of the Bible, natural elements, knowledge of astrology, mythology, and Platonic themes. Here is a brief indication of the most recurring symbols in the Tarot of Marseille.

- **Angel**: Messenger of the Divine.
- **Animals**: Instinct.
- **Beard**: Virility and courage. When it is present in older figures it indicates wisdom and spiritual authority.
- **Belt**: Element of separation between the upper and lower parts of the body; namely, reason and instinct.
- **Bust**: The material part is symbolized by the chest, the instinctive part by the belly. A richly decorated bust may signal specific qualities of the person in the area where the decoration is present.
- **Cloak**: Protection, but also isolation.
- **Collar**: Separation between the head (thoughts) and the body (emotions and sensations).
- **Columns**: Duality: masculine and feminine, love and hate, action and reception; finding oneself among the columns means occupying an important position.
- **Dress**: A protection, cover, the role of the wearer.
- **Flower**: Associated with the idea of center and the soul, it also refers to the transience of things and is tied to the passivity of the feminine principle.
- **Hair**: Strength and vitality.
- **Hat**: Connected to the thoughts of the wearer; it suggests the social role and is a symbol of protection.
- **Head**: Will, command; if uncovered, it corresponds to non-authoritarian figures.
- **Leaves**: Happiness, prosperity, the whole of the community; the active energy of the masculine principle.

- **Mask**: Man's ability to identify with the characters he represents, and thus the roles he plays in society.
- **Neck (uncovered)**: Simple communication between the mental and physical planes.
- **Nudity**: Candor, purity, authenticity. Freedom from conventions and superstructures.
- **Scepter**: Dominion, power, authority.
- **Throne**: Stable power.
- **Wand**: Link between heaven and earth.
- **Water**: Element of purification and regeneration, it represents life.
- **Wings**: Ascension and spirituality (they represented intelligence for the Ancient Greeks, and the spirit for the Christians).

NOTE: At the base of the symbolic architecture of Tarot cards are four figures: the Center, the Circle, the Square, and the Cross. The Center represents the One, the First Principle, the Absolute. The Circle indicates unity, eternity, perfection and the cyclic flow of time. The Square expresses the stability of matter, space and concreteness. The Cross is the symbol of orientation in space, of concentration and diffusion, it unites space and time, heaven and earth.

COLORS

Among the many versions of the Tarot of Marseille, the most widespread ones use a chromatic scale limited to a few essential colors. Below are the general meanings of the different colors. However, various card manufacturers have often used these in different ways.

- **Flesh color**: Human beings and physical, concrete reality.
- **Yellow:** Vital energy, solar intelligence, divinity.
- **Red**: Active energy (masculine). It is the color of blood, passion, and action in the world.
- **Blue**: Passive, receptive energy (feminine). Connected to the sky and to the depths of the sea, on the psychic level it represents the spirit and thought.
- **Green**: Nature and all that is in progress.
- **Brown**: Matter, solidity and all that is permanent.
- **White**: Immobility, absence of action, wisdom, purity and infinite possibilities.
- **Black**: Shadow, night, the end of things but also what defines them (it is used for the outlines of the figures).

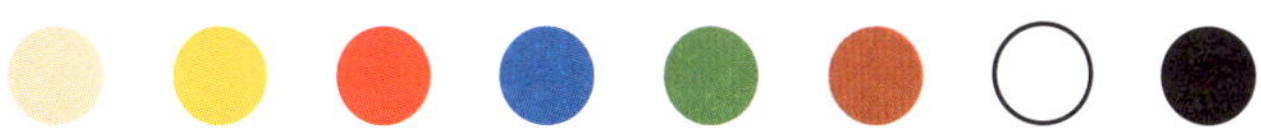

POSTURES

The characters portrayed in the Arcana are "alive" and assume specific positions making gestures to which we can attribute meanings. The orientation of the Arcana proceeds from left to right relative to the reader. As a rule, our left corresponds to the past, while our right represents the future. Therefore, in the interpretation, one must pay attention to the orientation of the figures and characters represented in the cards.

· **Arms**: *They are the visible expression of actions.*
The left arm symbolizes the passive and receptive side of the personality, while the right arm is the active one linked to will. If the arm is lowered, we can assume that the action has already been completed or that there is an impediment to act; if the arm is raised it may indicate a relationship with divinity and the ability to capture heavenly energies. Finally, the arm placed on the belt may represent the will to dominate instincts.

· **Legs**: *Indicate realization through action.*
If the legs are in a stable position, the action can proceed; if the legs are crossed, it expresses waiting and stasis.

· **Feet**: *Express the intention of the character.*
In general, the position of the feet expresses the direction that the person is taking. If a foot is lifted from the ground, it indicates a departure or a decision. When no decision has been taken, the feet go in opposite directions.

THE TAROT MISLEADS US

If we look at the cards of the Tarot of Marseille – especially at the Major Arcana – we sense that we immediately understand the action that a character is undertaking, an element of the composition or the very nature of the image itself. However, if we then focus on the details, we become less sure. Perhaps we see a woman who looks pregnant with a prominent Adam's apple (the Empress – Arcanum III); a stretched bow that, in some versions, has no cord and is therefore potentially unusable (the Lovers – Arcanum VI); a wagon with two horses and wheels placed sideways (the Chariot – Arcanum VII); a graceful looking foot with an excessive number of toes (Strength – Arcanum XI)... and so on, with many other examples. Why did we focus on these aspects? This is the true greatness of the Tarot of Marseille: nothing is as it appears to be. No card has an unequivocal meaning per se; they cannot be understood and interpreted using only reason, relying on concepts read somewhere: we must rely on our intuition, and on our sixth sense that the Arcana challenge us to use. Because everything is also the opposite of everything.

UPRIGHT CARDS OR REVERSED CARDS

Generally, it is believed that the meaning of the Tarot changes according to whether it is upright or reversed in a card reading, and that when the card is reversed it may indicate an intensification of the meaning, either by excess or deficiency. In the case of the Emperor (Arcanum III), for example, he could represent a person who is too authoritarian or who cannot make himself respected. Although we are used to thinking in terms of contrast between good and evil, no Tarot card has only positive or negative meaning. The direction we draw from it depends on how we approach the suggestion that comes from the card, and from the mental openness or closed-mindedness with which we place ourselves before this revelation. Having said this, the meaning of the Arcanum with respect to the question we asked of the Tarot will be given by its position relative to the other cards in the spread.

Upright Card

Reversed Card

NEGATIVE CARDS, POSITIVE CARDS

Do only positive or only negative cards exist? If we take for example the Tower (Arcanum XVI), does its coming out always represent a disaster? The answer is no. Each event or situation portrayed by the Arcana has within it both a positive and negative meaning. Just think of the saying, "when a door closes, a window opens." This is because the Arcana, communicating through a spread or individually, can assume characteristics that confirm, accentuate or negate the meaning of a card, depending on the situation or the question asked by the consultant. It is for this reason that, in the profiles of the Arcana, we have chosen to use a description that takes into account a basic interpretation, followed by its opposite. In this way the cards' indications can be drawn in a way free of conditioning.

CHAPTER THREE

THE MAJOR ARCANA

The 22 cards of the Major Arcana represent the great events (internal or external) of life, the fundamental aspects of our personality and of the people we may meet. They provide an in-depth view of the relationship with ourselves, with others, and our desires and expectations. As we mentioned previously, they can be considered as the main stages of a journey (ours) through the joys, the difficulties, the decisions, the people, and the situations that we encounter on the journey of existence. As in the Game of the Goose, the stages lead to the achievement of the final goal even if, as the progressive numbering of the Tarot indicates, we do not turn back, as indeed happens in life. Scattered among the Major Arcana there are numerous references to the Minor Arcana: swords, wands, cups as well as pentacles. This demonstrates that the Arcana are all connected and communicate in a subtle way amongst each other in a constant play of associations. Should one or more Major Arcana come up in a card reading, this indicates that the topic about which we are posing the question is very important: these cards suggest which path to follow which can be further specified by the Minor Arcana that are found in the spread. If no Major Arcanum turns up in a card reading, this could mean that the topic we are asking about is not so important or is not well placed. The Major Arcana can also be used on their own to read the cards: They suffice to allow us to understand the situation that is important to us in its general outlines.

DESCRIPTION OF THE MAJOR ARCANA

In the following pages the 22 Major Arcana are described in detail with particular attention to their peculiar characteristics. Their interpretation and the symbology linked to the card can thus be discerned. In each profile of an Arcanum, the name of the card is followed by a question with two often antithetical words, symbolizing the ambivalence that each Arcanum represents: nothing is only bad just as nothing is only good.

Each profile is divided into the following sections:

Interpretation: Where the core significance of the Arcanum is analyzed through its various meanings.

Questions: Their task is to stimulate intuition through visualization and active imagination.

Keywords: Where the fundamental terms that outline the card are indicated.

Symbols: Where the main symbols are examined and described.

Message: An indication that may be useful as a response.

LE MAT

I
LE BATELEUR

II
LA PAPESSE

III
L'IMPÉRATRICE

IIII
L'EMPEREUR

V
LE PAPE

VI
L'AMOUREUX

VII
LE CHARIOT

VIII
LA JUSTICE

VIIII
L'HERMITE

X
LA ROUE DE FORTUNE

XI
LA FORCE

XII
LE PENDU
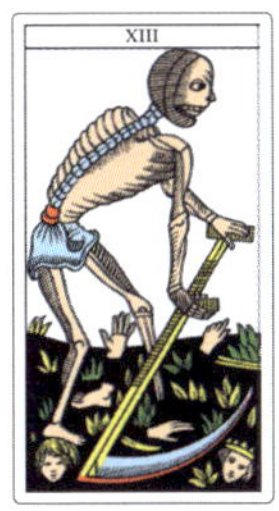
XIII

XIIII
TEMPÉRANCE

XV
LE DIABLE

XVI
LA MAISON DIEU

XVII
L'ÉTOILE

XVIII
LA LUNE

XVIIII
LE SOLEIL

XX
LE JUGEMENT

XXI
LE MONDE

LE MAT

0
THE FOOL

The main character looks like a wanderer, who carries a saddlebag on his shoulder, while holding a stick in one hand. He faces our right. Behind him is a dog, or perhaps a wild cat, that seems to touch his thigh. From an opening or tear in his pants you can see the skin of his leg. Hanging from his belt and around his neck are small bells recalling those worn by ancient court jesters. In the background is a simple landscape with alternating plants and earth. It is the only Arcanum without a number.

Genius or buffoon?

INTERPRETATION

The Arcanum represents man proceeding along the path of evolution through the stages of existence; as we mentioned before, since the card has no number, it can indicate the moment before the start of the journey or the moment after the end. It tells us about a new phase of life in which we can start from scratch, exploring new paths in search of experiences, without having to worry about what will happen. This occurs, for example, when we decide to change jobs or cities without knowing what awaits us and, despite this, we hit the road. The animal that accompanies him represents instinct, which can be helpful to us in our most difficult moments, an invitation to let go of reason and control, giving space to our nature without being blocked by the role we think we have in society. This is to allow our creative energy the freedom to express itself. **Or**, it could encourage us to be prudent, reminding us that we are proceeding in a superficial, rebellious, or irresponsible way, without taking into account our moral or material obligations; it may represent our fear of madness, the lack of self-control, the inability to respect the rules.

QUESTIONS

What is he carrying in his sack? Where does he come from? Where is he going?

KEYWORDS

Creativity, enthusiasm, freedom, lightness, adventure, madness, innocence.

MESSAGE

Entrust yourself to the unexpected. Nurture your freedom.

1 · The hat: Reminiscent of the headgears of the court buffoons and the Phrygian cap, emblem of wisdom, vitality and freedom also used during the French Revolution.

2 · The sack: It could contain knowledge and experiences that we all carry with us. A baggage – heavy for some, light for some others – which contains our history and that which we consider fundamental for our life.

3 · The clothing: Like that of a jester, colorful and partially torn, it indicates his disregard for social rules. The collar is decorated with bells, making his passage flagrant as it happened in the past for all those excluded from society, be they lepers, artists or saints.

4 · The animal: It is our instinctive side, which sometimes helps us act with courage, and sometimes pushes us to an excess of impulsiveness.

I
LE BATELEUR

I
THE MAGICIAN

The card depicts a young man standing in front of a table. On his head is a wide brimmed hat that dominates the top of the card, and he is wearing colorful and garish clothes. In one hand he holds a wand, in the other a small sphere. There are several objects resting on the table: coins, cups, dice, knives, and what seems to be a bag. He is facing us, but his head is turned and the eyes are looking to our left. We cannot see the fourth leg of the table, which rests on a barren ground with a few tufts of grass.

Skill or manipulation?

INTERPRETATION

The Arcanum represents a start, the beginning of all things and man's ability to dominate nature. We have a character in action, with a 'toolbox' in front of him. He tells the story of our youthful enthusiasm, the courage to act knowing we have the necessary resources. It could suggest that we are at the beginning of something potentially auspicious. For example, if we are thinking of starting a new business, it could advise us to act without further hesitation and move forward. It may also indicate a young or very lively character, skilled in the ability to talk and act, in creativity, charm and craftiness: the objects on the table refer to talents and one's ability to manipulate them for their own benefit. The fourth missing table leg makes it clear that one needs a lot of skill to keep the situation under control. **Or**, it could be describing someone who has all the tools and conditions with which to act, but lacks the initiative required; it may assume the negative traits of a trickster magician, an unscrupulous conjurer, an immature or unreliable character: for example, a new partner, a business partner.

QUESTIONS

What or who is he looking at? What are the objects on the table for? How will they be used?

KEYWORDS

Beginning, youth, skill, security, charisma, cunning, ideas.

MESSAGE

Act without hesitation.

1 · The hat: Reminiscent of the number eight on its side, symbol of infinity, it indicates the power of thought, which can go in every direction.

2 · The wand: Magical and powerful par excellence. It is turned upwards, representing the link between heaven and earth and the ability to transform supernatural energy into concrete acts.

3 · The table: It is the world of action, or the plane of reality, in which we manifest the most obvious part of ourselves, while the rest remains hidden. We only see three table legs, which seem to indicate the three worlds in which he acts: physical, intellectual and spiritual.

4 · Objects: All four suits of the Minor Arcana are present: the containers symbolize the Cups, the knife the Swords, the coins the Pentacles, and the wand, of course, the Wands. The dice might be there to remind us of Tarot's ancestors.

II
LA PAPESSE

II
THE HIGH PRIESTESS

The Arcanum depicts a mature woman, dressed in several layers of imposing clothes and with a papal tiara on her head which goes beyond the edge of the card; she is seated in front of us, but her upper body and head are turned toward our left. She has an open book in hand, but she is not reading. Behind her hangs a thick drape which takes up part of the background.

Knowledge or estrangement?

INTERPRETATION

The Arcanum represents the power of knowledge and of receptive feminine wisdom. It can tell us about a phase in which we give more importance to reflections than to action, tending to accumulate knowledge, without exposing ourselves too much to the world. It can also indicate our ability to guide others with our wisdom; a mature woman who knows how to listen and give good advice: a mother, a grandmother, a big sister, an experienced teacher, a wise, religious person. It may encourage us to be prudent and moderate; suggest that we be cautious when we are in the middle of something, that we must plan an important stage of our life, and thus time, patience and caution are necessary, as perhaps in the course of studying for an important exam which requires diligence. **Or**: It could represent a woman who is cold, austere, overly reflective and unaffectionate. A detached mother, for example, or a particularly tough teacher. It may also indicate our excessive passivity, a tendency to ruminate rather than to act, as in the case of the university student who continually postpones an exam for fear of not being sufficiently prepared. Finally, it may also refer to the estrangement from reality caused by devoting oneself to spiritual interests.

QUESTIONS

What is written in the book? Who or what is the High Priestess looking at? Who or what is behind the drape?

KEYWORDS

Wisdom, intuition, passivity, confidentiality, culture, mystery, coldness.

MESSAGE

Do not be in a hurry, learn the art of patience and wisdom.

1 · The tiara: It is also called the triple crown because it has three levels, which can indicate the three planes of existence (mind, body, spirit). This headgear was worn by important female mythological figures, as it represents the power of the Goddess: the creating power of woman.

2 · The cloak: Composed of several layers with an opening at the front, it signifies the willingness to offer the truth and knowledge symbolized by the open book.

3 · The book: It represents the knowledge we must draw on, without however clinging to it (the High Priestess looks elsewhere).

4 · The drape: It prevents the layman from seeing the knowledge safeguarded by the High Priestess. According to some interpretations, it may conceal the columns of a temple.

III
L'IMPÉRATRICE

III
THE EMPRESS

The card represents a woman of power, whose rank is made evident by the crown, the scepter and the shield. She is facing us, seated on a throne with a seatback resembling two wings; her gaze is turned toward our right. With one hand she presses the scepter to her belly, which is so prominent as to make her appear pregnant. At her side, with her other hand, she holds a shield with an eagle looking in the same direction. In some decks there is something at her neck that resembles an Adam's apple.

Creativity or dullness?

INTERPRETATION

In the Arcanum ideas become fruitful, to the point that the card can indicate an actual pregnancy; it describes an action that has already begun and is now ready to bear fruit: while the Magician acted from the waist up and the High Priestess hid herself from the rest of the world, the Empress seems proud to show herself. It could represent a woman who is very sure of her abilities, who is searching for a prominent place in society and who knows how to assert her authority. For example, we could expect a career advancement; the relationship that we have begun is becoming more serious, 'official'. It could be the representation of an important woman, such as a wife, or indicate ourselves in the role of partner of an important person. **Or**: We can become insecure, superficial or too careless. We do not master power well, and this can make us appear petty and opportunistic. It can also indicate sterility (not necessarily physical, it could be a creative block) or rejection of motherhood. It can represent a female figure who holds an important position (for example a boss) who perhaps tends to obstruct us.

QUESTIONS

What does she rule over? What is hiding in her lap?
Why does she hold both the shield and the scepter tightly?

KEYWORDS

Fecundity, important person, authority, practicality, decision, power, intelligence.

MESSAGE

It is time to achieve. Come out into the open and show the world what you are.

1 · The throne: It is linked to material aspects, but also spiritual ones as it seems to be surmounted by two wings.

2 · The crown: It symbolizes the strength of intellect and creativity that transforms thoughts into concrete actions.

3 · The scepter: It consists of a globe and a cross, indicating an alliance between temporal and spiritual power since, traditionally, royal authority is a divine emanation.

4 · The shield: It expresses royal power and the ability to defend oneself. The eagle indicates foresight and recalls intellectual authority: it is turned toward the left, mirroring the eagle on the shield of the Emperor (Arcanum IIII). The eagle appears in the World (Arcanum XXI) in which it represents the apostle John and the suit of Swords.

IIII
L'EMPEREUR

IIII

THE EMPEROR

In the card a mature man is resting on the throne without sitting down completely. His face is in profile, facing our left, while his body is turned three-quarters. He has a crown, a bushy beard and a large necklace. It is not clear if he is about to sit down or get up. With one hand he holds the scepter, while with the other he touches his belt. Below, at the base of the throne, rests a shield depicting an eagle, mirroring that of the Empress. The ground and a tuft of grass make one think of an outdoor landscape.

Authority or rigidity?

INTERPRETATION

The Arcanum represents power and material solidity. It can describe a phase of stability on the material or sentimental level (a permanent job or a consolidated relationship) or represent a mature male figure, who performs a role of power (a head of an office, an influential political figure) or plays an important role in our existence (a father, a partner perceived as mature). It also encourages us to reflect on our ability to make decisions with confidence regarding our life, without letting others do it for us. It may be telling us to focus our attention on a goal or on our role; it may remind us that we are important and we should not underestimate our impact on the world. **Or**: The Emperor may represent an immature, fragile, undecided man, or one who abuses his power. It can encourage us to pay attention to the material aspects of life that we are neglecting. For example, we are so happy with our role that we forget that an improvement is within our reach. The excessive need for stability could damage us, making us lose important opportunities. Finally, it reminds us that too much security can lead to boredom.

QUESTIONS

What is his power based on? Where is the throne located?
What will he do the moment after?

KEYWORDS

Stability, authority, concreteness, decision,
material power, paternity, strength.

MESSAGE

You are the master of your life. You have the power and
the authority to conquer your material stability.

1 · **The gaze**: It indicates dignity and the ability to look beyond.

2 · **The scepter and the shield**: The globe and the cross upon the scepter indicate power over the material world. The shield on the ground, with the eagle looking in the opposite direction to the one on the shield of the Empress, indicates intelligence subjected to material needs.

3 · **The necklace and the belt**: Dominion over emotions and instincts.

4 · **Crossed legs**: They seem to form the number four and can refer to the cards of the Hanged Man (Arcanum XII) and the World (Arcanum XXI); they are also similar to a cross and express the highest nobility, which consists in judging earthly matters with divine help.

V
LE PAPE

V

THE POPE

In the card we see a Pope, who is the main character, defined by his tiara and by the scepter on top of which is a triple cross. He seems to be blessing two (or perhaps more) clerics who are below. His gaze is turned toward our right. There is a noticeable disproportion between the size of the Pope and that of the characters below, who appear very small though being closer in perspective. Behind the Pope there are two columns, perhaps a part of the throne on which he is seated.

Mercy or severity?

The Arcanum represents spiritual power as a means of transmitting principles. It depicts a mature man, whose authority does not reside in material power but in that of the spirit: a sage, a priest, a guru, a therapist, a teacher, a philosopher. In any case, it indicates a figure who is important to us, a patron or a very protective father. Referring to the origin of the word 'pontiff' (as he who builds bridges), it can represent a figure able to act as an intermediary between two worlds. It may describe the ability to make our wisdom available to others, by giving good advice or by teaching. It can indicate our openness to spirituality after a period in which we were more attentive to concrete issues. Finally, it can symbolize a celebration (for example, a marriage) or a religious vocation. **Or**: The same character can become authoritarian and abuse his position by acting in bad faith. For example, a guru who becomes too attached to the benefits that derive from his role (money, charm); a very shrewd and unscrupulous politician. Finally, it may indicate a situation in which we lack deeper values, for example, a relationship based solely on sex.

QUESTIONS

What are the protagonists saying to each other?
Which of the characters do you see yourself in?
Where does the scene take place?

KEYWORDS

Spirituality, rite, vocation, guide, wisdom, goodness, conformism, mediation.

MESSAGE

Wisdom has value when it is shared.

1 · The two columns: Severity and mercy; they can represent the two pillars of Solomon's Temple, the first Jewish temple.

2 · The tiara and the processional cross: The tiara indicates the ability to direct one's own thought through material, psychological and spiritual dimensions; the cross with the three shafts refers to the ability to guide through the three theological virtues: Faith (dogmas), Hope (prayer) and Charity (benevolent action)

3 · The hand gesture: It refers to benediction, and suggests the transmission of knowledge and granting of grace; also, an invitation to follow the path of the heart. The glove with the cross indicates purity and harmony between the elements.

4 · The clerics: They can represent the two ways to access knowledge: actively and passively; or even the two different ways to address spiritual authority: prayer and supplication.

VI
L'AMOUREUX

VI
THE LOVERS

In the Arcanum a young man is between two women: an older woman and younger one. Above is a winged child shooting an arrow (the Roman god Cupid), inside of what appears to be a solar disc. But it is not for certain, as in some editions of this card the bow is without its string making the action impracticable. The young man in the middle is looking toward the older woman but seems to lean toward the other, while his feet point in both directions. Among the characters we notice a rather ambiguous intertwining of hands: it is not immediately obvious to whom they belong.

Choose or renounce?

INTERPRETATION

The Arcanum represents the ability to distinguish, and refers to a choice to be made before Cupid shoots his arrow, or rather before someone else decides for us. It can refer explicitly to feelings and a love triangle to be resolved, for example, by choosing between a partner and a lover. It can encourage us to open ourselves to love, especially if we are at the beginning of a relationship and are hesitating for fear of suffering or committing ourselves. It can indicate the need to make a professional choice, for example between a safe but uninspiring activity and a risky one that attracts us. It can also describe a rivalry between mother-in-law and daughter-in-law where the man is the object of contention. Finally, it can indicate a mother who blesses the union between two young lovers or who seeks to hold back the son: the possibilities are endless. **Or**: The necessity to choose becomes indecision, blocking, laziness. Both on the sentimental and on the material level, it can indicate a situation that has been dragging on for some time. We do not have the clarity needed to get out of an impasse. It could also represent our feeling inadequate regarding a situation that we find too stressful, or perhaps we feel listless, not very enthusiastic about how we are living, in our relationships or at work.

QUESTIONS

Who are the characters? Where does the scene take place?
How will it end?

KEYWORDS

Choice, trust, love, indecision, beauty, pleasure, balance.

MESSAGE

To choose means to live. Even the absence of choices is a choice.

SYMBOLS

1 · Cupid: The winged god, dressed as a child, is able to pierce the hearts of gods and mortals with his arrow; it represents the classic "love at first sight".

2 · The young man: Inexperience, ingenuity, but also vital energy and passion.

3 · The two women: They evoke the legend according to which the mythological hero Hercules found himself at the crossroads between Vice and Virtue. The garlands on their heads represent fruitful and changeable nature: the leaves are linked to rationality, the flowers to sentiment.

4 · The heart and the lower abdomen: One of the two women seems to be touching the heart, which is considered the seat of feelings and reason, the other is touching the lower abdomen, home to material appetites and sexual instincts.

VII
A.M
LE CHARIOT

VII
THE CHARIOT

In the card a richly dressed person – a prince, king or leader – is on a square chariot surmounted by a canopy and equipped with two horses that seem to be going in opposite directions. He is facing us but his gaze seems to reach beyond us and the horizon. Behind, two wheels are perpendicular to the wagon. In one hand he holds a scepter, while the other rests on his side. Two masks adorn his armor, one on each shoulder.

Stay or go?

INTERPRETATION

The Arcanum is the emblem of the ability to elevate ourselves, and describes an action we wish to undertake. It can describe a journey, an adventure or a situation in which we are called upon to reveal ourselves. It is an activity that yearns for recognition by others: for example, an actor who after a long apprenticeship is on set to shoot his first film. The Arcanum also represents determination, courage of those who know what they want and how to obtain it, but also the ability to combine reason and instinct to obtain a concrete result and to triumph. It can mean that a transfer will prove to be favorable. If we are uncertain whether to change city to make a change in our career, the Chariot invites us to action. It could suggest a profession related to transportation or an artistic profession such as in theater or cinema. **Or**: It can indicate the absence of dynamism, the inability to find a direction, or the difficulty in reconciling different aspects of our life, represented by the two horses: for example, we have different interests among which we do not know how to choose and we remain firmly in doubt. It may indicate an excessive self-assurance that does not rest on a solid base.

QUESTIONS

Who is the leader? Who is leading who?
What does this portrayal refer to?

KEYWORDS

Success, journey, exhibition, responsibility, control, determination, independence.

MESSAGE

Guide your triumph, no one can do it in your place.

1 · The columns: There are four columns, indicating stability and making up what in ancient times was called "The Chariot of Victory", set up for those leaving or returning victorious from battle. The canopy may indicate protection from external influences and royalty.

2 · Armor and masks: The suit of armor protects the chest indicating control of emotions; the masks on the shoulders refer to the roles we assume and could indicate rationality and instinct.

3 · The balustrade: Like the Magician's table, it hides the lower part of the leader from the observer. It indicates the detachment of the figure from that which surrounds him: only the socially acceptable aspect can be seen.

4 · The horses: They represent two opposite aspects of human beings (masculine and feminine, reason and instinct), our task is to find a balance between them.

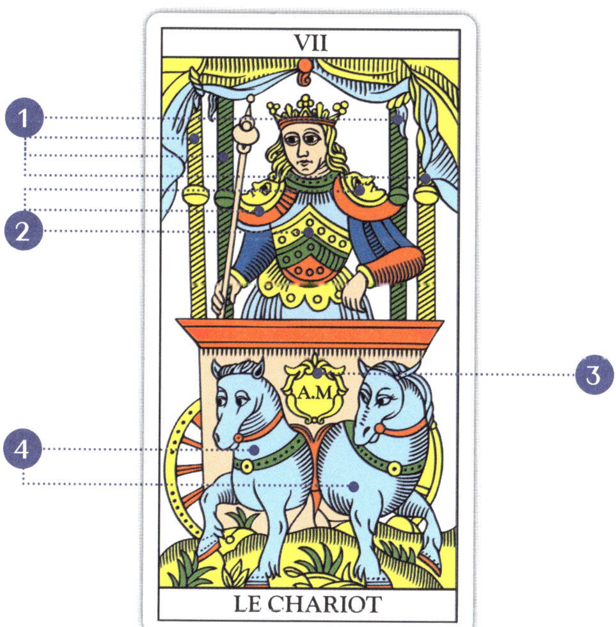

VIII
LA JUSTICE

VIII
JUSTICE

In the Arcanum a mature woman sits on a throne whose back is supported by two small columns; the high back conceals what is behind; her posture and gaze are both directed toward us. She wears a hat in the form of a semicircle, which culminates in a small crown, and a large necklace of braided gold. In one hand she holds a set of scales, in the other a sword.

Dictate or mediate?

INTERPRETATION

The Arcanum expresses the need to find balance between opposites and refers to fairness and impartiality. It could refer to a situation (a divorce, a trial) or a decision whose outcome will depend on the ability of the person who judges (a magistrate) to be objective and fair. It asks us to look inward to understand if we have acted according to our conscience: the result will depend on how we behaved. For example, if our question concerns a promotion at work, Justice will answer yes, as long as we deserve it. Finally, the Arcanum invites us to carefully evaluate the two possible ways to obtain justice: asserting our reasons with force, through the sword, or measuring scrupulously every action so that the needle of the scale is always in balance. It can be a judge, a notary, a diplomat or an authoritative law figure. **Or**: It can refer to legal problems, mishaps, but also our difficulty to be objective and reasonable, due to a tendency to apply double standards; it can indicate an excess of severity and rules, a strict person, obsessed with the fear of making mistakes or an erratic person.

QUESTIONS

Who is she? What is her judgment based on?
When does she use her sword and when the scales?

KEYWORDS

Balance, rigidity, harmony, law, logic, virtue, impassivity.

MESSAGE

Do you deserve that which you desire?

1 · The headgear: It is golden to symbolize the solar clarity of divine origin, and culminates in a thin crown to indicate the royalty of the character and to emphasize the authority of her role as impartial judge. Sunlight clarifies confused ideas and illuminates existence.

2 · The necklace: It is also golden, it expresses the close link with the solar dimension and therefore with the forces of good.

3 · The scales: It refers to moderation and balance for the capacity to weigh and evaluate every situation well.

4 · The sword: The ability to divide everything equally, but also the implacability in punishing the wicked; the tip pointing upwards refers to the divine origin of this power.

VIIII
L'HERMITE

VIIII
THE HERMIT

In the card an old man, wearing a thick coat with a hood, seems to move slowly, leaning on a stick; he is in profile, looking forward toward our left. In his raised arm he holds a lantern that illuminates his path. The card has no background except for a strip of land that can be glimpsed below.

Wisdom or isolation?

INTERPRETATION

The Arcanum indicates wisdom in which truth is found, symbolized by an elderly sage who carries out his search in solitude. It may lead us to think about a time in which we feel the need to gather within ourselves, temporarily moving away from the racket of the world in order to go alone looking for something or someone (an answer, a person, a place). It can represent a grandfather, a spiritual guide, a therapist or the wiser part of us, on which we must rely. It could be advising us to be patient, steadfast, prudent, that it is better not to fall into the fray. **Or**: It can highlight the tendency to close in on ourselves, out of shyness or selfishness. It can indicate that we should not talk too much, nor seek constantly the company of others, let alone act impulsively; it may warn us about those who present themselves as guides. It can represent a person who has remained alone unwillingly; a condition of widowhood or the end of an important relationship for which we are unable to give ourselves peace. Finally, it can represent the spasmodic search for company in the crowd, but without succeeding to soothe our sense of marginalization, feeling alone in the multitude.

QUESTIONS

What does his cape hide? Who or what is the lantern illuminating? How is the terrain on which he walks?

KEYWORDS

Wisdom, prudence, solitude, austerity, silence, meditation, humility, misanthropy.

MESSAGE

Search only for the truth.

1 · The beard: It expresses virility but also wisdom. It is a typical attribute of the ascetics, of the old sages of every spiritual tradition, and symbolizes the renunciation of every form of vanity.

2 · The hooded cape: It is a symbol of protection and privacy. The hood can refer to the ability to keep the thoughts secret.

3 · The stick: It represents the search for stability and the prudence with which we need to move forward in life. Like the wizard's wand, the diviner's stick or the king's scepter, it is also a symbol of power, for its ability to vertically connect earth and sky.

4 · The lantern: It symbolizes the inner light, the search for truth, the light of reason that distinguishes the sage. It recalls the hourglass which in ancient times represented Kronos or Saturn, god of Time, traditionally associated with this card.

X
LA ROUE DE FORTUNE

X

THE WHEEL OF FORTUNE

The card depicts a wheel with six spokes connected to a crank, on which we find three strange creatures: one in the act of going up, one in the act of going down, and finally a third one, equipped with wings, lying on top and wearing a crown, with a sword in hand resting on his shoulder. The wheel rests on a ground that seems to ripple.

Randomness or destiny?

The Arcanum represents the alternating of human events. Everything is transitory: we cannot hold on to any certainty. It would be interesting to ask ourselves with which element of the card we identify. If, when we see the card, we feel stable and secure but ready to defend ourselves like the animal at the top, it is important to know that we could go down at any moment. Or, perhaps we're climbing like the animal on our right, in this case the card describes, for example, our opportunity to rise the higher level, which we identify as the arrival of our hopes; maybe, we identify with the downhill animal, when circumstances lead us to leave something that gave us a sense of security. In general, the card can indicate a cycle in perpetual motion: the classic spinning wheel, like the extraction of numbers in a lottery. It makes reference to the classic 'stroke of luck', to those circumstances that lead us, even by chance, to reach a certain position. **Or**: It can describe a stroke of bad luck, an unpleasant snag, the end of a lucky streak. It can indicate the difficulty of relying on destiny, the tendency to control every aspect of life, or even an addiction to gambling.

QUESTIONS

Who is turning the crank? In which animal do you recognize yourself? How would you intervene on the wheel?

KEYWORDS

Destiny, luck, outcome, chance, change, conclusion, cycle.

MESSAGE

Accept that which you cannot control
and find the right time to act.

1 · The Wheel: It is one of the most ancient symbols and recalls the perfection of the solar disc, the cycles of nature, the eternal flow of life, the foundation to which everything is continuously born, grows and dies.

2 · The climbing animal: Expresses the attempt to conquer the summit; for some it represents Hermes, the messenger of the gods for the Greeks, and Anubis, the Egyptian god of death. In this double role it would symbolize a link between the world of the living and the afterlife.

3 · The descending animal: It represents the moment in which we abandon certainties and get in touch with our dark sides; it has been equated to two characters: the demon of Greek mythology, Typhon, and Seth, Egyptian god of evil and chaos.

4 · The animal at the top: It symbolizes an Egyptian sphinx, the mythological being which represents mystery and enigmas. It could represent a momentary state of equilibrium or a block that prevents the wheel from moving, or finally, the precariousness of power.

XI
LA FORCE

XI
STRENGTH

In the Arcanum a woman wearing a wide-brimmed hat keeps the jaws of a beast open with her hands, seemingly without effort. Her face is serene and her gaze seems to be directed elsewhere, not toward the animal; her body is facing our right. She wears a cape and a long gown from which the tip of a strange bare foot can be glimpsed.

Courage or control?

INTERPRETATION

The Arcanum indicates the courage that wins over brute force: the struggle for victory that can be achieved if we succeed in subjugating strength, and not be dominated by it. It can indicate physical and psychic strength, the ability to manage energies in a balanced manner without being carried away by our instinct; if, for example, we are in conflict with our partner or with a friend, this card invites us to not let ourselves be taken over by emotionalism. It can suggest that we have the resources to perform an act of courage or to overcome a fear; it urges us to dare, to 'take the bull by the horns', finally facing a situation that terrifies us. It describes an intelligent and determined person; it may be associated with professions that have to do with animals: vets, trainers, or the circus. It is also the ability to defeat arrogance, for example by responding in a balanced manner to provocations. It also represents inner strength, spiritual beauty and the power of a smile. **Or**: It can indicate the inability to tame one's instincts, the tendency to yield to outburst of anger; it may suggest that fear or an excess of self-control are preventing us from expressing our emotions. It can describe a phase in which we feel particularly vulnerable and respond to situations in an aggressive or passive way. Finally, it can represent an angry or weak person with whom we have to deal.

QUESTIONS

What is her gesture for? What would happen if she let go?
What name would you give to the human figure and to the beast?

KEYWORDS

Courage, discipline, energy, instinct, mental clarity, fear, strength.

MESSAGE

Courage is not an abuse of power nor an absence of fear, rather the ability to tame one's instincts.

SYMBOLS

1 · The hat: As in the Magician, it represents the power of thought, capable of expanding infinitely.

2 · The cape: It protects from external influences, it conceals and at the same time is a symbol of nobility and passion.

3 · The hands: They move gently yet decisively and firmly, as if to indicate the importance of gauging our gestures.

4 · The beast: It symbolizes instinct, but also sovereignty and power. In this card it could indicate not only our instinctive side but also the arrogance of those who believe themselves to be strong.

XII
LE PENDU

XII
THE HANGED MAN

In the Arcanum a man hangs by one foot from a beam between two trees whose twelve branches have been cut. His body and gaze are directed toward us, while the free leg is bent behind the other. His hands are behind his back, while at the base of the trees there are two tufts of grass. Despite the position, the man appears well dressed: his clothes are neither crumpled nor upside down.

Elevation or sacrifice?

INTERPRETATION

The Arcanum indicates a moment of stasis, a phase in which one is doing nothing. It could suggest that we had to stop or wanted to stop, for example to take care of ourselves or of someone else; that it is necessary to detach from a situation and give ourselves some time off. It could indicate our propensity to sacrifice ourselves for the common good, in order not to renounce our principles. The man hanged by his feet – a situation in which he cannot or does not want to do anything – is forced by circumstance to look at the world upside down: this position reverses his point of view and perhaps allows him to observe new or different things. **Or**: It may suggest an excessive tendency to sacrifice, risking to block ourselves, as in the case of the 'savior syndrome'. It can also indicate the presence of a victim complex, or the inability to remain still because one is taken by too many activities. It encourages us to reflect on all the situations in which we chose not to act, reminding us that even not doing is still doing something. In some decks there are coins falling from the pockets of the Hanged Man to remind us that the choice to stay still has a cost.

QUESTIONS

Who tied him up? If he were free, what would he do? What does he see upside down?

KEYWORDS

Sacrifice, expectation, surrender, gift, spiritual elevation, reversal of perspective, victim complex.

MESSAGE

Look at things from different points of view.
Sometimes it is better not to act.

SYMBOLS

1 · The beam: It is the point of balance between two trunks that can indicate two opposing aspects of existence.

2 · The rope: It could represent a bond between the Hanged Man and reality, or perhaps what keeps him alive and ties him to people and things.

3 · The posture and appearances: His crossed legs can indicate both a punishment and a voluntary sacrifice: they recall the cross, the Emperor (Arcanum IIII) and the World (Arcanum XXI). The free leg seems to imply the possibility to climb down. His appearance recalls that of the Magician, emblem of action, moved to inactivity.

4 · The cut branches: They symbolize the need to eliminate that which is useless, but they also refer to the symbology of 12 (the twelve zodiac signs, the twelve labors of Hercules, the twelve apostles). This correspondence associates the Hanged Man to the sacrifice of Christ on the cross.

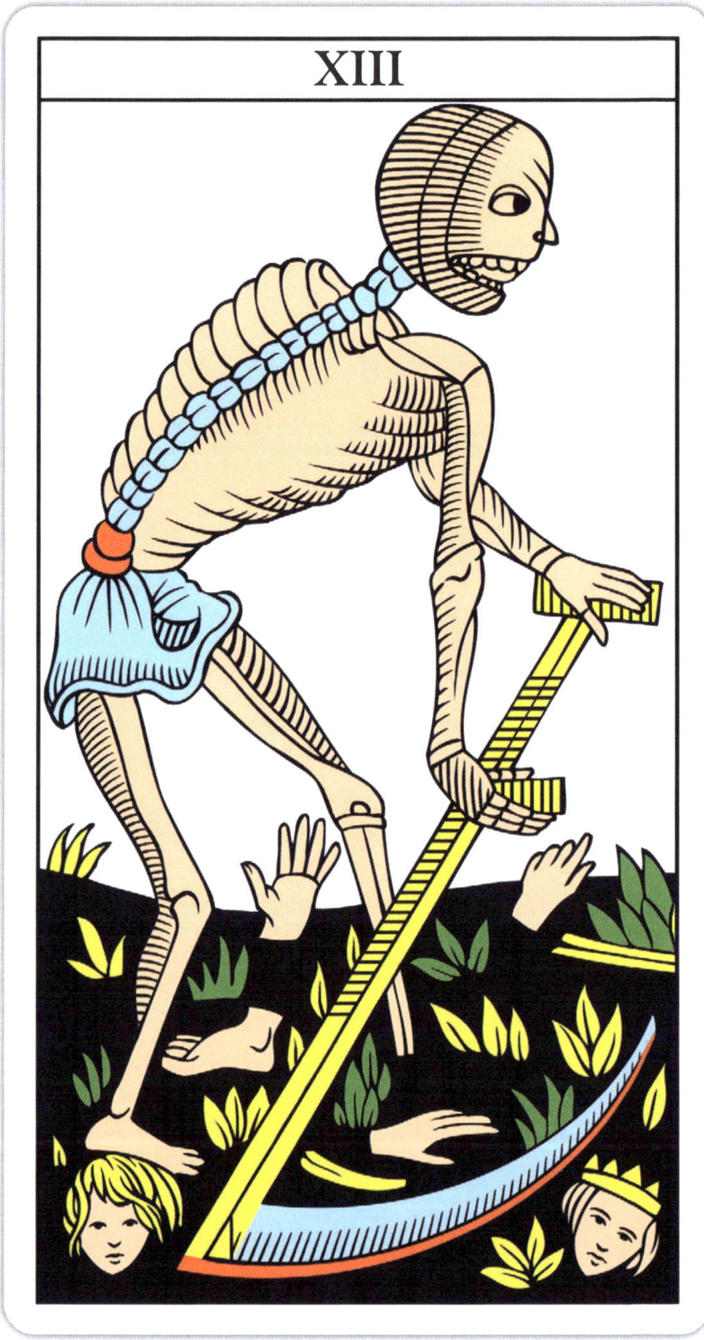
XIII

XIII
THE NAMELESS ARCANUM

In the card, a skeleton holds a scythe with both hands, looking toward our right (the future). Beneath him, a dark ground on which we see tufts of grass and flowers, bones, hands, feet and two heads: one seems to belong to a woman, or to a child, the other to an adult, perhaps a king as he is wearing a crown. From the image it is not clear if one of the cut feet belongs to the skeleton. In most decks the Arcanum has no name.

Death or rebirth?

INTERPRETATION

Traditionally associated with Death, the Arcanum marks a phase of profound change and radical transformation. If we have stayed too long in a relationship, that is now worn out, it is time to sever the tie. If we are still immature, it is time to make ourselves autonomous. In short, the card encourages us to put an end to a certain way of being, identifying that which we truly want and that which instead should be left to die out. However, when we cut something, we might be forced to make do without a part of us (the missing foot of the skeleton). The card also expresses a sense of rebirth given that on the ground there are plants as well as human parts: we don't know if they have been cut or belong to someone who is emerging from underground to new life. The skeleton can encourage us to manifest our essence, without superstructures, taking care only of what is truly important. Finally, the card recalls the classic meaning of death as a leveler, joining kings and commoners. **Or**: It can represent a static period, difficulty to change, out of fear or laziness or, on the contrary, a need to destroy for the sake of destroying, which prevents you from building anything. It can also indicate our fear of change; the tendency to pessimism and to cling to situations that no longer belong to us.

QUESTIONS

Who do the heads, the bodies, and the bones belong to?
Who was the skeleton? Why is he scything?

KEYWORDS

Radical change, transformation, cutting,
return to the essential, loss, inertia, death.

MESSAGE

It is necessary to cut the dry branches to make new life bloom.
Go to the essence of things.

1 · The skeleton: It is the most durable element of the body, and in the card it represents our essence. His posture reminds that of the Fool, the card that has no number, while Arcanum XIII has no name, perhaps because in ancient times death could not be named.

2 · The scythe: It is used to cut clean, but also to harvest grain. It is therefore a potentially deadly tool, but capable of guaranteeing the harvest, and thus the nourishment and perpetuation of life.

3 · The human remains: They refer to the path of birth, growth and death that unites us all.

4 · The ground: It is dark, but the presence of plants seems to refer to natural cycles: next to the remains of what has been, there are signs of renewal.

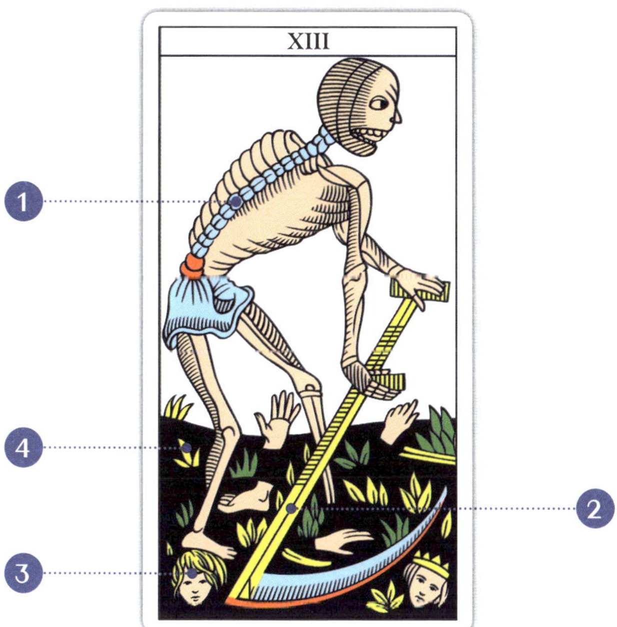

XIIII
TEMPÉRANCE

XIIII
TEMPERANCE

In the card, a female figure with angel wings and a flower on her forehead pours a liquid between two amphorae that are almost at the same height. The figure faces us, but the upper body seems to be turned to our left, while the lower body to our right. In the background we can glimpse a barren landscape with two tufts of grass.

Balance or confusion?

INTERPRETATION

The Arcanum represents the balance and eternal play of matter's energies; it can refer to the idea of attention, patience and measure, as well as the ability to reconcile diverse situations. It can represent a thoughtful person, capable of applying him or herself with great dedication and expertise. It can also symbolize modesty given that this angelic figure seems to be doing a rather humble task. Just before an important exam, or when faced with numerous deadlines, it reminds us to have faith in the fact that we will be able to achieve our goal if we plan carefully, act in moderation and give ourselves the right time. Given that it follows Arcanum XIII, it may symbolize a recovery after a difficult period; a positive figure capable of protecting and reassuring us. It reminds us that 'in medio stat virtus': virtue stands in the middle. **Or**: It can signal a disorderly, intemperate action, a lack of trust in our resources. It can warn us against the tendency toward fickleness: we might be too devoted to following the fashion and opinions of others, or too focused on only one thing and forgetting the rest. Finally, as the angel does not spill water on the ground from the two amphorae, it can refer to the idea of sterility and a barren land. It could indicate a repetitive task, which can be boring or fruitless.

QUESTIONS

What are the wings for? What would happen if the liquid spilled? What if she stopped pouring?

KEYWORDS

Balance, calm, healing, patience, harmony, dryness, stagnation.

MESSAGE

Be moderate and prudent: with patience you can accomplish difficult actions.

1 · The flower: Its shape, with the petals that surround the central corolla, recalls divine essence. It can also refer to nature, as seen in all its beauty and continuous change.

2 · The wings: They make us think of an angel, a messenger, an intermediary between God and humanity; it can indicate our ability to rise above human weaknesses.

3 · The amphorae: Associated with the feminine and the suit of Cups, they symbolize the ability to contain; according to some interpretations they refer to the miracle of the wedding at Cana, when Jesus transformed water into wine. In some decks they are of two different colors, symbolizing two opposing energies (for example, masculine and feminine).

4 · The liquid: It can represent water, understood as a vital female element (by way of association with the amniotic fluid) or even refer to the generative force of male sperm. The pouring of liquid may refer to the principle of energy conservation.

XV
LE DIABLE

XV
THE DEVIL

In the card we find an androgynous figure with both feminine and masculine attributes, with horned headgear on its head and wings like those of a bat. Its hands and feet look like paws. The figure is standing, its posture and gaze directed toward us, holding a sword (in some decks a torch) in one hand; it stands on a pedestal on which there is a rope that ties two strange naked creatures with tails and horned hats.

Power or slavery?

INTERPRETATION

The Arcanum often arouses apprehension because the Devil traditionally symbolizes evil and all that upsets and dismays, as opposed to the goodness of God. However, the Devil is also a figure that exerts great magnetic appeal because it represents power, money and seduction. It can describe a phase in which we feel a strong psychophysical energy and personal magnetism, and we attach much importance to our ego. It can portray a charismatic person, who tempts us with pleasure and who is able to seduce us: a partner or a boss who is able to obtain everything he wants from us, a relationship in which we feel deeply involved that transcends our will. The card refers to sexual desire as a strong link that holds two people together. **Or**: It can indicate temptations, selfishness, arrogance, ambition, excesses that risk damaging us. The ropes that bind the two creatures can represent a bond that keeps two people together unwillingly, an external force that dominates them (a great physical passion, a dominant supervisor at work, a marriage held up by an external force). Finally, it may concern an addiction, whatever form it takes.

QUESTIONS

In which of the characters do you recognize yourself? How do you feel in this situation? How could the two creatures free themselves?

KEYWORDS

Instinct, pleasure, ego, sexuality,
lack of self-control, charm, addiction.

MESSAGE

Learn to manage your power. Too much energy can dominate you, too little energy can limit you.

1 · The headgear: It has the form of a helmet, traditionally associated with Hades, Greek god of the underworld (Pluto for the Romans). In some cultures, warriors wore horned headgear to transfer animal strength and vitality onto themselves.

2 · The wings: They recall those of a bat, an animal that evokes the world of shadows and the occult.

3 · The sexual attributes: Androgynous, they symbolize ambiguity, but also sexual power and union between masculine and feminine principles.

4 · The two creatures: They could represent the lack of awareness of human beings, slaves of passions or of attachment to the material realm. According to many interpreters, they are a male and a female.

XVI
LA MAISON DIEU

XVI
THE TOWER

The card shows a crenellated tower with three windows. Above, a flame – perhaps lightning or a fire – it is not clear if it is going into or emanating from the uncovered building; below, two human figures upside down seem to fall or flutter down to the ground in opposite directions: you see the whole figure of one and only the upper body of the other. The sky is filled with many small colored spheres; the ground is barren and dotted with tufts of grass. At the foot of the Tower are two shapes that resemble bread or stones. We don't know if the Tower has a door. The Arcanum is called "La Maison Dieu" (the House of God).

Collapse or revelation?

INTERPRETATION

The Arcanum represents the ephemeral and fruitful constructions of man; traditionally associated with the Tower of Babel, it is considered by many to be a negative card because it is connected to unforeseen events, the collapse of illusions, and to divine punishment for human arrogance. The upper battlement of the Tower resembles a crown and the fact that it is knocked over reminds us that human power cannot compare to Nature or the divine. The Tower is an impenetrable place, so the card could suggest a release from something that held us prisoner, such as a secret, mistaken beliefs or from someone who was blocking us; what might seem like a catastrophe will turn out to be a positive event, because we are finally free. It can also indicate a strike of lightning out of the blue or an unexpected revelation. The name of the card can refer to the fact the God is everywhere, even in the Tower. **Or**: The card can represent a collapse: of illusions, psychophysical health, of a work situation, a relationship, a friendship. It can symbolize a condition of real or metaphorical imprisonment, an event that precipitates things and forces us to change; it can advise us to tell the truth, however difficult that may be. Finally, it can be a reference to humility in the face of an excess of presumption: what seems solid can collapse.

QUESTIONS

Who or what took the roof off the Tower? What is the mood of the characters? How do you feel inside or outside of the Tower?

KEYWORDS

Sudden event, change, liberation, presumption, collapse, fall, captivity.

MESSAGE

Do not cling to any false certainty.

1 · The fire: It is a symbol of purification and transformation. Understood as lightning, it can recall the divine power and punishment.

2 · The tower: For some a phallic symbol, for others the image of the Tower of Babel, it can represent family, home, the human body, or a man–made enterprise (for example, a company).

3 · The colored spheres: They could represent fragments of sky, coming to earth from the destruction of the abode of God and the angels.

4 · The three windows: According to some they indicate the planes of being (physical, mental and spiritual), according to others they are the eyes and the "third eye" (thought). They also represent the part of us that opens to the outside world, being 'filters' that allow light and air to enter a building.

XVII
L'ÉTOILE

XVII
THE STAR

In the Arcanum is a naked woman, kneeling on the bank of a stream; she seems very focused while pouring a liquid from two amphorae. The content of the first amphora ends up in the stream, that of the second is poured onto the ground. In the background, a sky dotted with seven stars and a larger central star; in the barren landscape we see two trees: on one of them rests a black bird.

Hope or illusion?

INTERPRETATION

With this card begins a sequence of Arcana that refers to astronomical elements. The Arcanum invites us to follow our calling and have faith. It is connected to living in harmony with the cosmos (the stars), of which human beings are an integral part: in this sense it is the card that, more than any other, refers to astrology. The Arcanum contains several references to all four elements: the stars (Fire), the sky and the black bird (Air), the amphorae and the pool (Water), the ground and the trees (Earth). The woman is naked, symbolizing a condition of authenticity and freedom from constraints, but also the ability to get naked in front of our own weaknesses. It can indicate a situation in which we feel at peace with ourselves and do something that is in tune with our most genuine desires and aspirations. It can be a reference to the most beautiful expressions of human creativity: music, visual art, fertility. Finally, it can refer to the act of following the flow of life, without seeking to obstruct it. **Or**: It can represent the circumstances in which we feel 'out of place', uncomfortable, and we don't let our creativity flow freely. It can also indicate a lack of trust in fate and in the future; the tendency to bare ourselves even when it could prove inappropriate.

QUESTIONS

Why is the woman naked? What did she take off?
What is the liquid she is pouring used for?

KEYWORDS

Harmony, hope, beauty, foresight, desires,
disappointment, pessimism.

MESSAGE

Trust your lucky star.

1 · The stars: Traditionally, the stars are a guide in the night sky and the symbol of astrology. There are seven minor stars in the card, associated with the seven planets known since ancient times (the Sun, the Moon, Mercury, Venus, Mars, Jupiter and Saturn). Then there is a larger star, which according to some represents the Star of Bethlehem that guided the Magi to the hut where Jesus was born.

2 · Nudity: Symbolizing purity, authenticity, freedom from appearances and from the conventions of which clothing is an expression.

3 · The amphorae: In the Temperance Arcanum the woman, dressed, poured water from one amphora to another. Here, the woman, naked, empties hers with a gesture that can appear both generous and confident: the universe will know how to give back what she offers.

4 · The bird: It can symbolize communication between the earthly world and celestial world, or an opening toward other dimensions.

XVIII
LA LUNE

XVIII
THE MOON

In this Arcanum we find the Moon represented in one of its phases; inside a luminous circle a face is drawn whose profile is directed toward our left (the past). Drop-like rays seem to come from the earth toward the Moon; two animals are facing each other, with their muzzles also facing the Moon. In the background there are two towers. In the foreground, a stretch of water with a large crayfish inside.

Intuition or deception?

INTERPRETATION

The Arcanum recalls the symbolism of the Moon and represents the dreams that come to life with the complicity of the night, the sensibility, the emotions, the memories, the receptiveness and our instinctive side. It is tied to the feminine, to water, to the tides, to imagination, to fantasy, to dreams, to secrets, to nighttime thieves, to everything that is not clear and defined. It can symbolize a particularly receptive, sensitive and intuitive person. It can concern our need to keep a secret. It can refer to a good relationship with our female side, or in a strict sense, with women. The card also indicates imagination, intuition and memory; daydreams. Finally, our unconscious (the crayfish) in the depths of the mind. **Or**: It can indicate our insecurities and emotional dependencies; a rather shy, undecided, and at times slightly childish and moody character; a secret situation we are experiencing, a deception, a moment of confusion in which we struggle to see things clearly. It can also represent a female figure with whom we have an unclear relationship or, in general, a difficult relationship with women and the mother figure.

QUESTIONS

What is inside the towers? What are the animals doing?
If the crayfish could speak what would it say?

KEYWORDS

Mystery, secrets, intuition, hidden things,
feminine, ambiguity, passivity.

MESSAGE

Listen to intuition, make sure what is hidden comes to light.

1 · The moon: Nocturnal star in constant transformation, with its monthly phases it marks the stages of life and the tides, in analogy with the menstrual cycle. For this, and because it does not shine with its own light but reflects that of the Sun, it is associated with the receptiveness of the feminine.

2 · The animals: Perhaps dogs, they can refer to Hecate, lunar goddess of which they were faithful companions.

3 · The two towers: They can indicate the entrance doors to the two solstices, summer and winter that divide the year into two parts. The summer solstice takes place with the entrance of the Sun in Cancer, a sign dominated by the Moon. According to tradition, the incarnation of souls took place in Cancer through the "door of men"; the exit took place through the "door of gods" in the opposite sign of Capricorn.

4 · The crayfish: It refers to the zodiacal sign of Cancer, the first sign of water traditionally associated with the Moon and motherhood. It is situated in a pond, symbol of what is hidden and indistinct, like amniotic fluid.

XVIIII
LE SOLEIL

XVIIII
THE SUN

In this Arcanum we find the Sun and two young figures. The Sun is represented as a face that looks forward toward us, radiating the earth with colorful drops. Below are two half-naked figures wearing a collar, close to each other in a confident and complicit manner. In the background there is a low wall, in a barren landscape.

Clarifying or blinding?

INTERPRETATION

Complement of the Moon, the Sun represents the active male principle, creative intelligence. Here it indicates our vision of life, the energy we possess, vitality, and our qualities of loyalty, courage and generosity: it is also an expression of steadiness, stability and constancy. It can represent a clear situation, for example a happy marriage, a stable couple, a functioning society. It can also refer to joy, warmth, solidarity and harmony of intent. It can indicate a happy agreement, for example a contract that favors both sides equally. As in the card of the Devil (Arcanum XV), there are two beings below a dominant figure, but here they are unbound, their relationship is free and voluntary. Finally, a sentiment secured by external influences (the wall). **Or**: An excess of light can blind us. In a couple, it could mean that the two people are in such symbiosis as to exclude the outside world. The idea is reinforced by the image of the wall that seems to enclose the two figures. Moreover, an excess of heat can make us arid, it is the case of people who demand 'a place in the Sun'. Finally, the card can indicate a conflictual relationship with male figures of reference.

QUESTIONS

Who are the two figures? What is beyond the wall?
What might the Sun say?

KEYWORDS

Joy, light, clarity, love, friendship, blinding, isolation.

MESSAGE

Operate above board and respect others.

1 · The Sun: The diurnal star, it is one of the first symbols associated with divinity. Source of life, it symbolizes male energy, the light that defeats the darkness, the truth and intelligence that clarify every doubt. Its rays represent the power to give life and also to destroy it.

2 · The drops: They represent the divine energy that comes down to earth to bless and generate life.

3 · The two figures: They are naked, to symbolize purity, innocence, confidence. They could refer to the archetype of the Divine Twins (Castor and Pollux, Romulus and Remus, Euryalus and Nisus).

4 · The wall: It is an indicator of separation, delimitation. It can also symbolize the foundations on which to start building, or the wall atop a tower.

XX
LE JUGEMENT

XX
JUDGMENT

In this Arcanum we find a winged angelic figure emerging from a cloud, playing a trumpet to which a banner with a cross is attached. On the ground, a naked man and woman appear in prayer while a third figure, seen from behind, emerges from a tomb. The cloud seems to emit rays.

Rebirth or abrupt awakening?

INTERPRETATION

The Arcanum represents the divine summons, a rebirth, the awakening of our conscience toward a superior state. It can indicate our need to follow a vocation or to be reborn, for example by completely renewing our habits, interests, lifestyle, radically changing our profession or situation. It can allude to a completely new phase of our existence in which renewal is definitive and irreversible. The image resembles the Lovers (Arcanum VI), but this time the characters on the sides do not touch the central one, which seems to hunch toward the Angel. The Arcanum advises us that the time has come to undertake our path, without external interference. The card can also refer to a message or a call that engenders an important change. **Or**: It can indicate the inability to follow our calling, due to inertia or because we are overly subject to outside influences. It can warn us of our tendency to make judgments; it may suggest a difficulty in making decisions. It can refer to bad news; our refusal of happiness for fear of being disappointed, for example by avoiding a new relationship or accepting a new job.

QUESTIONS

Who are the three characters? Who is the Angel addressing?
Where does the call lead to?

KEYWORDS

Calling, vocation, renewal, awakening,
revelation, repentance, inertia.

MESSAGE

Follow your calling: do not fear judgment.

1 · The angel: It seems a clear reference to Judgment Day that will occur at the end of time, when the angel of God will sound the trumpet, resurrecting all mankind and, based on their actions, dispatch them to Heaven or Hell.

2 · The trumpet: It can represent the communication of an important message, the sound that awakens, the call to which one must answer. It has a flag with the image of a cross, symbol of cosmic order and balance between opposites, banner of the celestial army against the forces of evil.

3 · The characters: They can indicate the family triad, but also the three components of an individual: body, mind, and soul.

4 · The tomb: It is a symbol of metamorphosis, of death and resurrection. In the Christian tradition, Jesus rose from the tomb three days after his death, but also caused Lazarus to resurrect.

XXI
LE MONDE

XXI
THE WORLD

In this Arcanum we find a half-naked human figure facing us: it is partially covered by a veil, its gaze directed to its right, in its hands are two wands with an unusual shape. It is placed inside a garland, while at the sides there are four figures: a lion, an eagle, an angel, and a bull.

Realization or the end of a cycle?

INTERPRETATION

It is the arrival point of the Arcana. This card is the symbol of perfection reached at the end of a journey, thanks to the harmony and completeness between the different aspects of existence. It can represent the desired result that we manage to achieve after a lot of effort; the satisfaction of having achieved our goals, for example a long-awaited job, a degree, a pregnancy, a success that makes us feel fulfilled and that can bring us fame and glory. It can indicate the balance between the four aspects of existence (sentimental sphere, practical life, intellectual part, creative and sexual energy). The double masculine and feminine principle, merging into one androgynous being, renders us complete and balanced (the figure at the center of the garland). In this way we are the protagonists of the scene in our story which ends in triumph. Finally, it is the awareness of possessing all the elements that are indispensable to us. **Or**: It can refer to the inability to close a chapter of our life, an excessive closure in ourselves. It may suggest an imbalance in one or more areas of existence that make it impossible to feel satisfied. It can indicate something unfinished, stagnation. Finally, it can make us resistant to showing ourselves as we are.

QUESTIONS

How would you feel being the figure in the center? What are the objects in its hands for? What would the four figures at the sides say?

KEYWORDS

Fulfillment, happy closing of a cycle, achievement of desires, perfection, balance, fame, stagnation.

MESSAGE

You have reached perfection. It is time to start anew.

1 · The central figure: For some feminine, for others androgynous, it can represent the Anima Mundi of the alchemists, or the conclusion of the Magnum Opus. The crossed legs recall those of the Hanged Man, with the difference that the Arcanum XII is upside down. In the same way, the garland contrasts with the cut branches and the square surrounding the Hanged Man. This play of contrasts seems confirmed by the fact the Arabic numerals 12 and 21 assigned to the two cards are mirror image.

2 · The wands held by the figure: They represent the two polarities of existence: the active male principle and the passive female principle.

3 · The garland: It symbolizes the Cosmic Egg, the perfection of nature.

4 · The four beings: The Tetramorph, symbol of the four evangelists, the four elements, and the four suits of the Minor Arcana. The lion is Mark, creative dimension (Wands – Fire); the eagle is John, intellectual dimension (Swords – Air); the angel is Matthew, emotional dimension (Cups – Water); the bull is Luke, material dimension (Pentacles – Earth).

CHAPTER FOUR

THE MINOR ARCANA: THE NUMERICAL CARDS

While the Major Arcana describe universal principles, fundamental aspects of our character or that of those we may encounter, very important situations and what we must do in order to face them, the Minor Arcana provide specific information on the facts, transferring to practical reality what is expressed in a general way by the Major Arcana. Imagining that we are dealing with a novel, we can think of the Major Arcana as the protagonists and the Minor Arcana as the individual events and secondary characters who contribute to building and clarifying the story in detail. Alternatively, the Major Arcana are the plot, and the Minor Arcana are the individual episodes. Although the Minor Arcana resemble the cards of a normal deck, they present an interesting symbology which, if well interpreted, make it possible to analyze the contingent situation with greater clarity. As we have mentioned previously, the Minor Arcana are 56 in total, subdivided into four suits (Wands, Swords, Cups, and Pentacles) and are composed of forty numerical cards (ten per suit) and sixteen court figures (four per suit). We will now go into detail of the first group.

DESCRIPTION OF THE NUMERICAL CARDS

Here, the forty Numerical Cards that make up the Minor Arcana are described in detail, subdivided by suit. Each card is divided into the following sections:

Interpretation: Where the core significance of the Arcanum is analyzed through its various meanings.

Keywords: Where the fundamental terms that outline the card are indicated.

Message: An indication that may be useful as a response to a question.

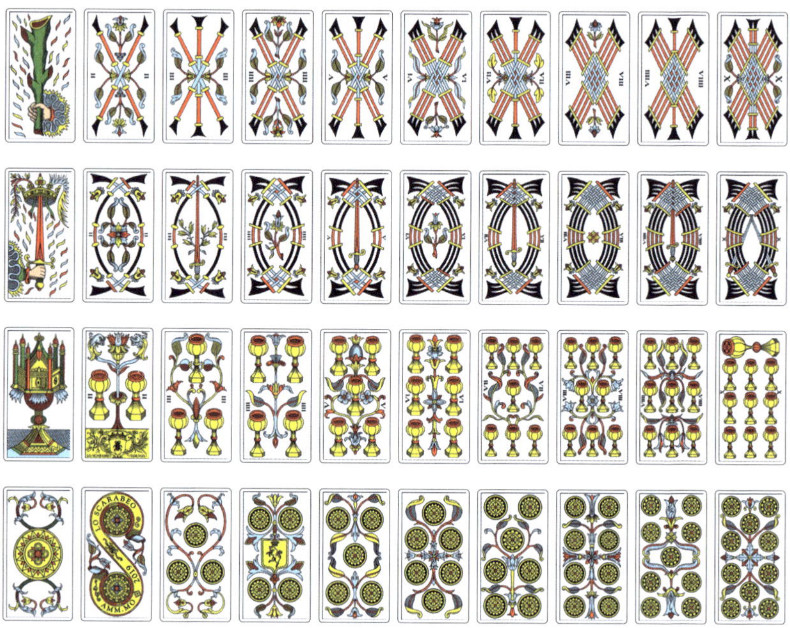

WANDS

Wands are associated with masculine energy, as their elongated, almost phallic form reminds us; with the element of Fire, that acts as a catalyst, making us concentrate on the meaning of things, and with the zodiac signs Aries, Leo and Sagittarius. With regard to the physical world, the shape of the wands recalls that of trees, as if to indicate a link with the world of nature, the wands can also be used as a weapon (for example, as a club or cudgel) to fight obstacles. It is the suit of laborers, of those who perform tasks that require a lot of physical energy, and in general of those who, for one reason or another, need to exploit their own strength. We find the tree or wood in several mythological/religious tales: the tree of knowledge of good and evil, from which Adam and Eve took the forbidden fruit; the burning bush where Moses met God; Daphne, the nymph loved by Apollo who turned into a laurel tree to escape him. The cards of the suit of Wands are energetic: they give the idea of action and can refer to difficult tasks and jobs. Having several in a spread means giving much importance to practical activity and to personal commitment.

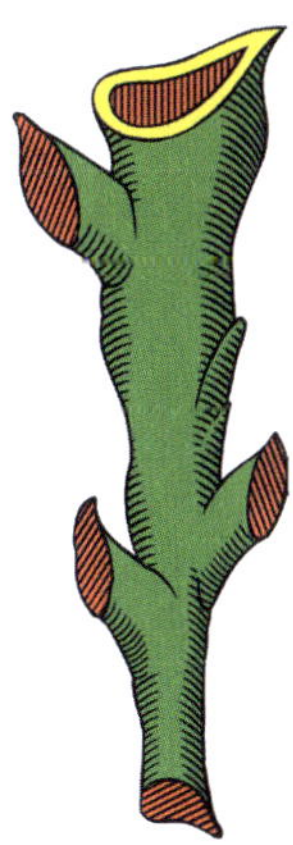

ACE OF WANDS

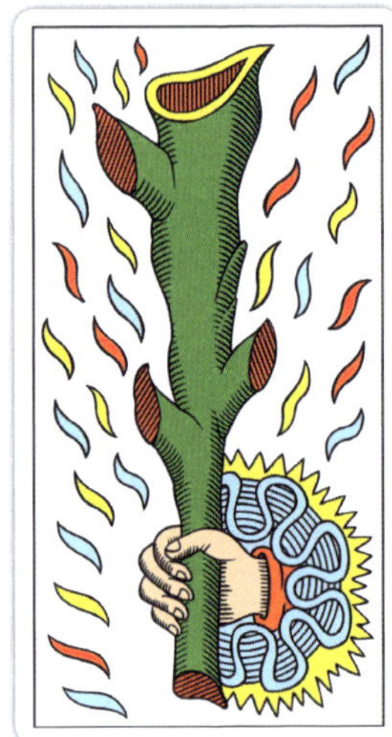

A hand emerges from a circular cloud-shaped opening to our right, holding a stick vertically that appears hollow inside and has some cut branches on the sides. In the background, in a corner, many colored shapes appear as rays of energy, and seem to suggest a sun behind the clouds.

INTERPRETATION: It represents the fertile power of the masculine, creativity and abundance, and is a good omen for any beginning, from the conception of a child to the start of a work activity. It can symbolize a new relationship, a new passion, an important experience that is about to begin. For example, if we have decided to work for ourselves, the Ace of Wands encourages us to continue along this path. We feel energetic, creative, capable of doing great things. It can also symbolize physical resistance: with the stick we can defend ourselves or even attack. **Or**: It can indicate a loss of power, a moment in which energy or trust are lacking, a surrender, the end of something. It can also lead to a difficulty in reaching a goal because we feel confused, undecided; we prefer not to act out of laziness or fear. It could indicate that we feel drained and we need rest to recover; that we are misusing our vital energy.

KEYWORDS: Creation, beginning, masculine energy, invention, conception, postponed beginning, discouragement.

MESSAGE: Trust your ability to create something new.

TWO OF WANDS

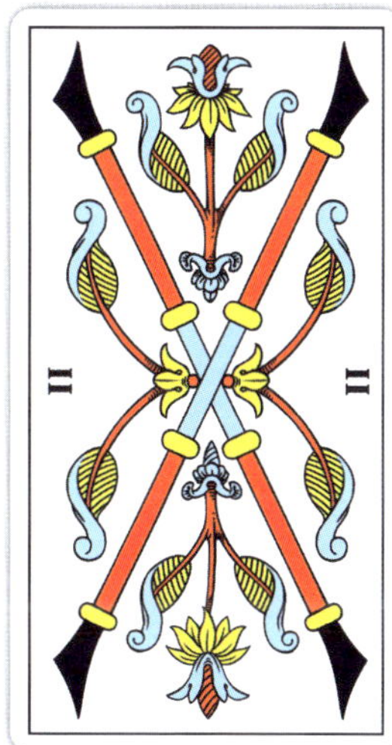

Two wands cross each other forming a perfectly symmetrical X. Two flowers are arranged at the top and bottom, along the side edges are two pairs of plants; the symmetry is complete, both up and down and on the sides.

INTERPRETATION: Here the energy of the Wands meets the Two, opening up to comparison with one different from itself. The crossing between the two wands can represent the union or the clash that can occur when two strong energies meet. The card can suggest the ability to show courage in the face of an obstacle or an unexpected event. That which happens when, for example, we are flanked by someone with whom we must collaborate: it may give birth to something new, the result of the contributions of both. It can also indicate a future expectation, the desire for an activity to come to fruition, but from a long-term perspective. In general, it can describe maturity and responsibility but also knowing how to evaluate the pros and cons prior to action. It also suggests a worthwhile union, or an alliance that can prove successful. **Or**: It can highlight an excessive ambition or the inability to overcome an obstacle. Expectations for an agreement or an activity are high and generate doubts, indecision, or difficulty in assessing risks. Finally, there may be a problem working in a team.

KEYWORDS: Idea, association, maturity, courage, ambition, indecision, selfishness.

MESSAGE: Every action must take into account the reaction that it is able to generate.

THREE OF WANDS

To the two crossed wands of the previous Arcanum, a third is added in the middle. This third element replaces the flowers of the Two, while the plants at the sides remain perfectly symmetrical.

INTERPRETATION: The two wands seem to have produced a new reality, hosting a third element that can symbolically refer to trade and creativity. The action is unfolding, the desire expressed by the previous card here becomes the will of realization: the flowers of the Two have become the third wand. It can indicate a concreteness rich in creativity that can be used in the artistic, inventive, craft or entrepreneurial fields. It can symbolize a sudden intuition that grows to become a winning project. Finally, the card can refer to evolving situations: for example, associations, collaborations couples who are thinking of getting married or having a child. **Or**: It may indicate a disappointment relative to a project in which we had believed, an unreliable or unproductive person; a rude awakening with respect to something whose premises seemed positive. Finally, it can signal a lack of practical sense that prevents us from realizing our projects.

KEYWORDS: Creativity, openness, new project, hope, resourcefulness, lack of concreteness, disappointment.

MESSAGE: It's time to act. The ideas and projects should be put into practice.

FOUR OF WANDS

The wands are arranged in pairs, crossing each other. The space occupied by the central wand of the previous card is filled here with two bloomed flowers (while the flowers of the Two of Wands were still budding), but whose roots are cut and simple, while in the Two they were pointed and decorated. Moreover, the two flowers this time are different, no longer identical. Finally, the calyxes that contain the side leaves are open.

INTERPRETATION: The Four refers to what is real and tangible and indicates that the fiery energy of the Wands is given out in a constant manner. The card can be associated to events such as the harvest, a reward for your efforts. It can also symbolize a positive attitude, a stable relationship, the tranquility achieved in an enterprise and in that which you have worked for; peace, serenity, trustworthy and lasting friendships. **Or**: It can represent the end of a friendship, an unrequited love or one ended the moment we were called upon to commit ourselves, insecurity. It may suggest that too much stability has extinguished our passions, making us excessively rational or too preoccupied with expectations. Furthermore, it could indicate a sense of instability and confusion with respect to what we wish to accomplish.

KEYWORDS: Stability, reward after much effort, tranquility, important social and emotional relationships, maturity, dryness, insecurity.

MESSAGE: The moment has come to reap what you have sown.

FIVE OF WANDS

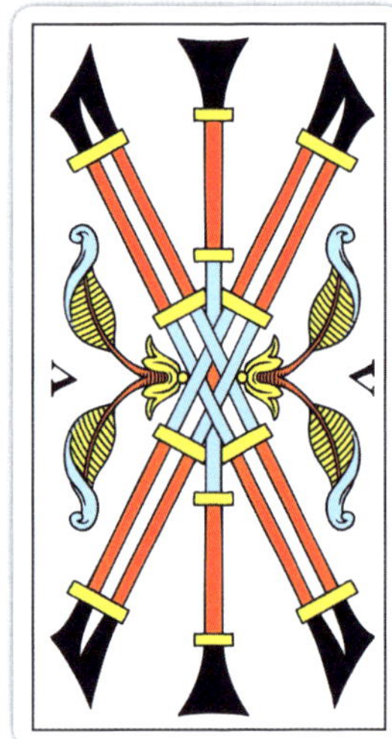

To the four wands in a cross, a fifth is added that replaces the flowers. The floral motif thus disappears again, while two symmetrical leaves remain on the sides, equal to those of the previous cards (except the Ace).

INTERPRETATION: The card can represent struggles and opportunities for competition that allow one to measure one's strengths, the ambition for growth in the workplace. It speaks of power clashes but also of successes. The card can suggest that in order to maintain what has been achieved, one must make sacrifices, change perspective. For example, a company that has always maintained a solid market position, faced with a new invention by a competitor, will have to take countermeasures and dare to do something new, in order not to risk falling behind or failing. The central wand could refer to an activity that needs to open up to new markets, including foreign ones. **Or**: It can indicate a defeat, a trick played on us, a betrayal, a deception or a fraud, an occasion in which we felt our dignity was hurt, like in a situation of workplace bullying. Events or situations that can hamper us, perhaps our own fear or a tendency to be a creature of habit, too stable.

KEYWORDS: Commitment, struggle, change of perspective, complexity, ambition, conflict, fear.

MESSAGE: It is not possible to remain still. We must dare to go further.

SIX OF WANDS

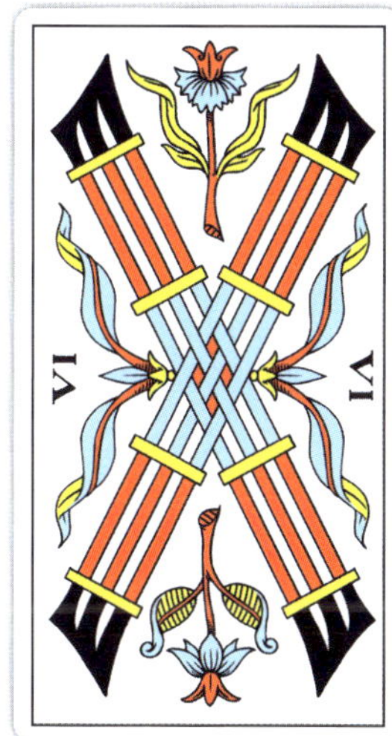

The wands, an even number again, are arranged in two pairs of three. At the top and bottom are two flowers that are different in each of their elements: petals, stem, corolla and leaves. On the sides are two floral decorations, identical and symmetrical, yet more elaborate than in the previous cards.

INTERPRETATION: The card can indicate overcoming difficulties, balance and vigor. It can also refer to a winning and altruistic attitude that allows one to achieve triumph thanks to sacrifice, or even success, good news, desires that are fulfilled. It may concern victories that seem to come effortlessly, but which are in fact a result of efforts made in the past. Everything comes easy. For example, at work we are entrusted with a new task that we have been waiting for for a long time; after waiting a long time we finally find the house we wanted at a reasonable price. **Or**: It may indicate news that is slow to arrive, uncertainty in business, loss of trust at work, obstacles to success, setbacks; it can put us on guard of our own vanity, for example when, after many successes, we convince ourselves of our merits. The card appears as an urging not to remain anchored to luck, beauty, power, success by encouraging us to accept their transience.

KEYWORDS: Earnings, advances, wishes come true, recognition, vanity, superficiality.

MESSAGE: Know how to revel in your successes by keeping yourself balanced between humility and pride.

SEVEN OF WANDS

Once again, the wands are odd-numbered, and house one more wand in the middle. The flowers disappear at the top and bottom, the two plants at the sides remain, similar in composition to those present in the Six.

INTERPRETATION: The number Seven, in the suit of Wands, describes those difficulties that have a stimulating effect as they push us to use energy and ability to overcome them. The card can indicate a specific person who is able to handle with ease even the most complex issues. It can refer to the safety of those who overcame obstacles in the past and know how to get around; a good debater, the choice of valid strategies and collaborators. It is a possible index of success, but not as immediate as in the Six of Wands; here we are talking about long-term success, which requires time and effort. **Or**: It can suggest the presence of enemies, a loss of opportunity, fears that can lead to defeat. It can signal our lack of determination, a sense of incompleteness and indecision, a lack of ability to tolerate frustrations, the feeling of wasting our energies in something that hesitates to take off (for example, a project that has been dragging on for some time).

KEYWORDS: Challenge, commitment, security, effort, determination, indecision, fear of failure.

MESSAGE: Learn to accept challenges as a stimulus to grow.

EIGHT OF WANDS

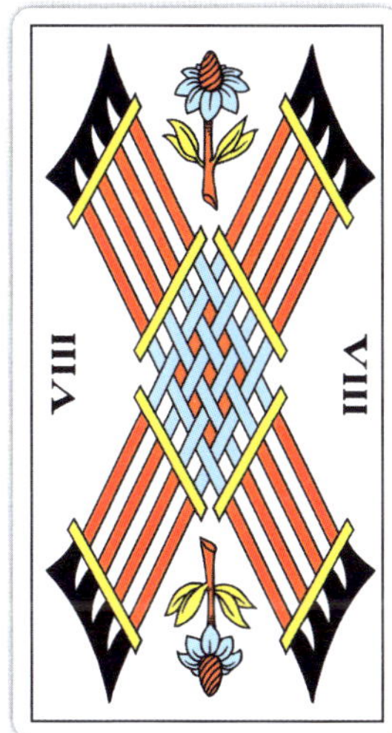

A perfect symmetry returns. The eight wands are arranged in two groups of four, at the top and bottom are two identical flowers.

INTERPRETATION: Eight is a number that expresses balance and represents justice and impartiality; in the Wands it is characterized by a strong dynamism. The card can describe strong and decisive personalities, as well as sudden events that lead to a quick solving of complex situations. It can represent travel or unexpected news. It can also refer to a phase of profound transformation that is important to learn to accept, for example a transfer or a move, capable of causing a change of work, friendships, habits. Finally, it can signal that a period of great sacrifice is finally giving the long-awaited fruits. **Or**: It can refer to problems in the family or with relatives, mishaps and delayed trips. It may concern a difficult period in relation to a specific objective, in which the need arises to take stock of our past actions to understand where we may have made a mistake, to what extent we have committed ourselves. For example, faced with a failure at work, it can invite us to reflect on the collaborators chosen, the energy dedicated, or the resources we had at our disposal.

KEYWORDS: Sudden progress, change, climax, dynamism, reflection, laziness.

MESSAGE: Embrace change, learn from past mistakes.

NINE OF WANDS

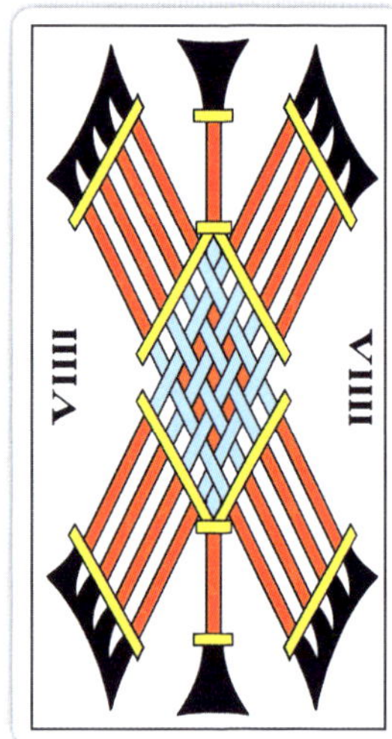

The ninth wand is placed in the middle, while the remaining eight are arranged as in the Eight. The two flowers at the top and bottom disappear to make room for the wand.

INTERPRETATION: The number Nine represents the ability to compromise, a particular maturity. In the suit of Wands, it can indicate the ability to open oneself up to knowledge and to leverage one's mental agility to cope with obstacles. The central wand can be the symbol of a single point on which one has chosen to concentrate. The card can describe attitudes that inspire trust, strength and balance. It may suggest that accumulated experience increases our responsibilities, but also our ability to manage them; it encourages us to act with foresight with people we trust at our side. For example, if we are about to start a particularly demanding undertaking, it may be appropriate to evaluate the people who will be part of it and leverage our experience, but also our maturity and ability to mediate between different needs. **Or**: It can describe a phase of distrust, closure, immaturity. We tend to think in a rigid manner and are not inclined to compromise, or we are dispersing ourselves between too many points of view regarding a question, rather than focusing on one goal.

KEYWORDS: Tenacity, maturity, solidity, mediation, discipline, responsibility, distrust.

MESSAGE: Don't be afraid of your responsibilities: turn them into a strong point.

TEN OF WANDS

Despite being an even number, it has an unusual division with respect to the previous cards: eight sticks cross each other in two sets of four, while the other two vertically intersect them. There are two symmetrical red plants on the sides.

INTERPRETATION: Ten represents the crystallization of energy and in this suit shows concentrated strength and power. The card can describe the obstinacy and tenacity of taking on many responsibilities. It is an Arcanum particularly related to work or home. It can symbolize the end for a new beginning, an enticing project, a great ambition and a willingness to self-realization. Finally, the card can suggest saving energy in view of some future projects that will require an even greater commitment. **Or**: It can describe a waste of energy in areas and in objectives that don't materialize; it can signal the presence of external pressures, urgent problems that need solving and require great effort. Too much work without achieving tangible results can generate stress and psychophysical fatigue, as well as the tendency to always say yes for fear of losing an important occasion.

KEYWORDS: Effort, commitments, new beginnings, success, pressure, fatigue, end.

MESSAGE: It is important to work hard to be successful, but it is equally important to accept the end of a cycle.

SWORDS

The suit of Swords represents communication, the struggle for independence, pride but also authority, aggressive spirit, situations of struggles and mental or verbal challenges. The Swords are associated with the element of Air and the zodiacal signs of Gemini, Libra and Aquarius. The sword has a double blade and expresses the duality of the rational element: the mind offers a more lucid understanding, and thus is able to create, but it can also turn itself into a sharp blade capable of hurting and destroying. It is the suit of the military, of nobility, of people who wear a uniform such as lawyers, policemen, surgeons, of journalists whose pen can hurt more than a sword, in general of all those who use physical or intellectual weapons to carry out their work. In the Marseille Tarot, the swords are curved and make us think of scimitars. The world of sacredness and magic is also linked to this suit. Symbol of warriors and power, the swords are generally depicted in the hands of kings and knights. In Christian tradition it is the weapon of Archangel Michael who kills the dragon. The tempering of the sword is the union of water and fire that generates air. The cards of the suit of Swords are the energy of thought: they give the idea of rational understanding and can refer to mental or physical duels. Having several in a spread means giving much importance to intellectual activities and challenges.

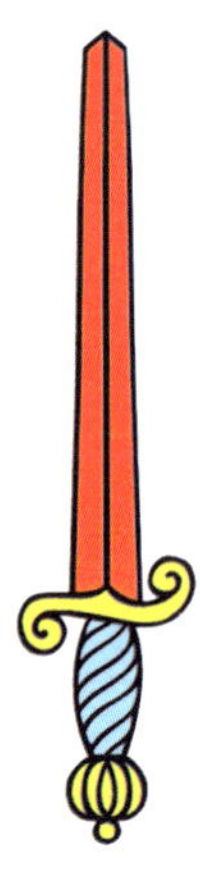

ACE OF SWORDS

A hand emerges from an opening to our left, holding a sword vertically. At the tip of the sword is a crown decorated with flowers, leaves and other decorations. One can see cut branches facing upwards, and another severed branch that seems to fall downwards.

INTERPRETATION: It can indicate a situation in which we must leverage our authority, a victory, decisions that lead to the success of projects; a passion, a conquest, a strong determination, a lucid intelligence able to lead us to reach our goals. It can also symbolize a particular sense of justice, charisma, impetus. It can indicate the struggle to distinguish ourselves in a company, relying on all our resources; cutting ourselves some slack; a period of great turmoil in which we must be mentally lucid. **Or**: It can describe a tendency to express one's ideas aggressively, an overbearing and tyrannical way of doing things. It can also symbolize an obstacle; weakness and mistrust in our intellectual abilities. Finally, it can describe a phase of overload or mental fatigue, in which we feel the need to not think too much.

KEYWORDS: Power, authority, conquest, intelligence, success, weakness, laziness.

MESSAGE: Trust your ability to distinguish, without abusing it.

TWO OF SWORDS

Two curved swords form an oval, in the center of which there is a large flower, accompanied by symmetrical plants. On the four sides, at the intersection of the swords, there are four flowers facing outwards, also arranged symmetrically.

INTERPRETATION: When the Two and Swords meet, it may be necessary to go through a period of reflection or even to take into account the presence of the other, learning to manage conflicts. In fact, it can describe opposing forces, disputes, but also a phase of truce, justice, order. We must learn to express ourselves clearly and to affirm our own needs, while listening to and respecting those of others. It is a process that requires balance and security. Finally, the card can allude to the fact that one can rely on trusted friends, or that one has been involved in an honest competition. **Or**: It can indicate unscrupulous actions, imbalance, conflicts caused voluntarily, lack of self-control. Situations in which no balance has been found; one is too argumentative or docile. True friends must be distinguished from those who practice flattery for their own benefit.

KEYWORDS: Balance, harmony, firmness, friendship, mediation, conflict, deception.

MESSAGE: Learn to say 'yes' when it's yes, and 'no' when it's no.

THREE OF SWORDS

A third sword is added to the two curved and crossed ones of the previous card, placed at the center of the oval with the tip pointing upwards. On the sides of the central sword are two crossed twigs, while at the four corners of the card there are the same flowers as seen on the Two.

INTERPRETATION: The third sword placed in the center can be considered an element of rupture in the balance between the two. This is why this card is often associated with misunderstandings and conflicts. It can represent something that breaks into our lives, questioning some aspect of it, for example the awareness that our relationship no longer works. It can also indicate a willingness to affirm one's own knowledge and one's point of view, which, however, is not sufficient; we must mature before launching ourselves: it may be the case of a project presented to important customers that has not been prepared with due care. **Or**: It can symbolize the end of a truce, but also a big obstacle that delays us or stops us from doing something. It can signal that we feel confused, worried; that we are inattentive about an important aspect of some matter that must absolutely be considered.

KEYWORDS: Distraction, opposition, error, removal, separation, delay.

MESSAGE: To mature is not the obstacle: it the condition for success.

FOUR OF SWORDS

The swords are divided into two pairs of two, forming an oval that encloses a flower bud, quite different from that on the Two of Swords. At the four corners of the card are the same four symmetrical flowers of the previous cards.

INTERPRETATION: The number Four expresses consolidation and a moment of stasis useful for rearranging ideas. The Arcanum describes a phase of mental and psychic recovery. It is necessary to gather ideas, define the details of a question, momentarily detach from the action and from external pressures to reflect in solitude. It can also describe the resumption of a relationship after a discussion, or convalescence immediately following an illness. Finally, it may indicate that we are waiting to prepare something that requires great precision and dedication. "The calm before the storm." **Or**: It can describe a phase of distancing or separation, a loss, a moment of forced loneliness, a phase in which we would like to have some time to think, but external stresses prevent it. Finally, it can warn against excessive perfectionism or, on the contrary, a tendency toward superficiality and impulsiveness.

KEYWORDS: Preparation, perfectionism, reflection, convalescence, solitude, impulsiveness, superficiality.

MESSAGE: It is important to stop and reflect, to measure one's words and actions.

FIVE OF SWORDS

As in the Three, a sword placed at the center is added to the oval formed by two groups of two swords, but this time it is not surrounded by plants. On the sides of the card are the four symmetrical flowers seen in the others.

INTERPRETATION: The fifth sword is a conflictual element, which can indicate the need to measure oneself against something important, for example a new challenge in which we will need to bring forth determination and courage. It can also represent a conflict that must be faced, for example in a couple, or a rivalry at work or in love that should not be seen as reasons to stop us, but rather as incentives to move us forward. Finally, the card may concern our striving toward higher ideals, the will to overcome ourselves, trying to give new direction to our thoughts. **Or**: It is possible to experience a defeat, having to face enemies, losses, betrayals; uncertainty about the outcome of a project. It can also signal an excessive idealism that pushes us to fight for a cause, making us lose sight of other priorities. Finally, it may indicate a moment in which we feel weak, mentally tired or fragile, unwilling to stand up or affirm our reasons.

KEYWORDS: Competition, conflict, conquest, rivalry, high ideals, weakness, defeat.

MESSAGE: Only by facing our rivals will we be able to grow.

SIX OF SWORDS

At the center of the oval formed by two groups of three swords is a cut flower in bloom, adorned by two leaves of equal size with a five-petalled flower plus the bud. At the four corners of the card we find the four flowers present in all the previous Arcana, except for the Ace.

INTERPRETATION: The difficulties encountered in the Five can be overcome; the moral and intellectual qualities appear in perfect harmony. The card can symbolize new hopes and opportunities, like travel, overcoming obstacles, and deserved triumph. It can also describe a period in which many ideas that could succeed are elaborated; the desire to go beyond the usual ideas by thinking something new; the curiosity that allows us to search and find different stimuli; a mental journey, the ability to daydream; meditation. A real journey to destinations that stimulate our curiosity. **Or**: It can describe the tendency to escape from our responsibilities; lack of perspectives; the tendency to be or perceive ourselves as a creature of habit. Finally, it may indicate a certain weariness, confused and aimless fantasies; a journey never made or that has not satisfied us.

KEYWORDS: Travel, reasoning, curiosity, reflection, fantasy, escape, apathy.

MESSAGE: Travel, with your feet or with your mind. Explore new worlds.

SEVEN OF SWORDS

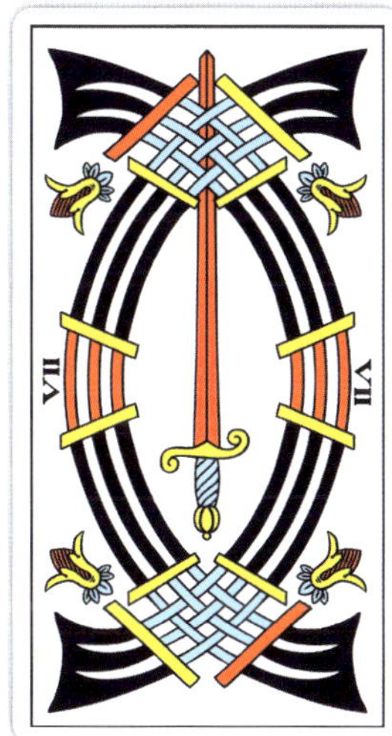

At the center of the oval formed by two series of three swords, returns a single sword, similar to that of the Five, because it has no decoration. At the sides of the card, once again, we find the four symmetrical flowers.

INTERPRETATION: This card describes the trials one must go through to acquire knowledge at the end of a path. Thoughts become lucid and practical: desires, new projects; we must use all our wisdom to transform our ambitions into concrete projects. The card invites you not to give up, even if at the moment everything seems wrong. It may be the case of a writer who sends a novel for the umpteenth time after being rejected by several publishers, without losing trust in his work: maybe this time will be the good one. **Or**: It can describe a sense of discouragement. It is a warning not to publicize our projects so as not to expose ourselves to gossip. Difficulty in accepting criticism and listening to the advice of others. Finally, it may describe a phase in which we cannot think in a practical manner or commit ourselves to actualize our ideas.

KEYWORDS: New projects, desires, hope, trust, practical ideas, gossip, unwelcome advice.

MESSAGE: Do not give up, stay calm, move on.

EIGHT OF SWORDS

The center of the oval, consisting of two series of four swords, is occupied by a simple flower without a stem, made of eight petals decorated with gems or berries. The pattern of the swords becomes more and more dense, while at the four corners there are symmetrical flowers.

INTERPRETATION: The stable nature of the number Eight does not reconcile very well with the mutability of the element of Air, and this causes a forced immobility. It can indicate a period of closure in ourselves and reflection, in which we need to recharge our energies to recover lucidity and enthusiasm. It can also represent the need to consider more aspects of the same issue calmly and carefully, without rushing to conclusions. For example, if we doubt the good faith of a friend, the card can urge us to evaluate our state of mind and the situation in the most objective way possible, before passing judgment. Finally, it can represent that healthy restlessness that in the future could push us to change some aspects of our life. **Or**: It can describe the awareness of living in a stagnating situation with the inability to overcome it; a crisis, betrayals, lack of ideas and joy. We feel restless and pessimistic about our situation; for the moment we feel we cannot do anything to change the state of things.

KEYWORDS: Reflection, pause, restlessness, crisis, fear, confusion, pessimism.

MESSAGE: Gather ideas and stop and reflect before acting.

NINE OF SWORDS

The central sword, which we find in all odd numbered cards, appears almost covered by the lattice of the two series of four swords that cross each other. Symmetrical flowers are present at the four corners.

INTERPRETATION: It can indicate a phase of inspiration, in which one wants to put one's intelligence at the service of high ideals, for example, a humanitarian cause. It can also represent a period in which one feels worried, or impatient with obligations and conventions; better not to be satisfied with easy answers: let's get to the bottom of our issues. It can also indicate a strong tendency to empathize and concern ourselves with the problems of others, especially those of our loved one, if we are a couple. It can be an indication of wisdom and maturity; the ability to look beyond. **Or**: It can indicate a phase in which we feel full of doubts. In this case, it can warn us that it is better to select the people with whom we surround ourselves more carefully, because our trust in them is rather low. It can refer to the fact that we feel remorse for something we have done in the past; that we have been deceived and now we tend to shut ourselves in for fear of new disappointments. Finally, it may encourage us not to close our eyes to problems and to face the facts.

KEYWORDS: Inspiration, depth, empathy, concerns, doubts, mistrust, isolation.

MESSAGE: To be idealistic does not mean to be vulnerable.

TEN OF SWORDS

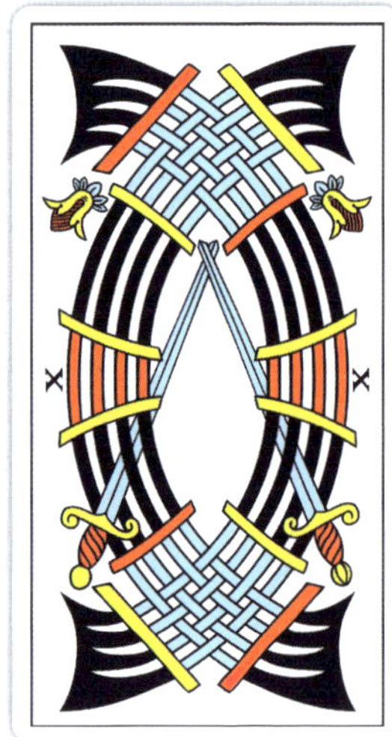

The oval is composed of two sets of four curved swords, while the remaining two are straight and crossed, as in a duel. Of the four symmetrical flowers present in the other cards – with the exception of the Ace – only two remain.

INTERPRETATION: It can encourage us to break a balance that appears perfect, in order to embark on a new path. We are responsible for making this change happen: it is up to us to grasp the swords as effectively as possible. For example, when we have given our all to a job, especially on an intellectual level, and now we need to recharge. It can also represent the need to measure ourselves with a great fear that prevents us from going forward but which, once overcome, will open up new paths for us. Finally, it can indicate an ability to observe things in a fair, objective way, knowing how to mediate between opposing needs. **Or**: It can encourage us to reflect on how appropriate it is to break a balance with respect to our usual way of thinking. It could also concern a certain tendency to argue, a conflict, a propensity to 'invade' the thought of others to impose our opinions. Finally, it could indicate a tendency to avoid conflict, intolerance, a lack of motivation for change.

KEYWORDS: Impatience, conflict, thinking outside of the box, change, intrusiveness, responsibility, search for new balance.

MESSAGE: It's time to think outside of the box and invent something new.

CUPS

The cards of Cups refer to feelings, situations of love, happiness, cheerfulness, spiritual and material fulfillment, personal relationships, the emotional sphere. They allow us to understand our deep motivations and encourage us to follow our intuition, to let ourselves go, to receive without necessarily having to give something in return. They also indicate deep feelings, memories, the past. It is the suit of artists, priests, sommeliers, those who have chosen a helping profession, such as coaches and counselors or social workers, in general all those who, for one reason or another, handle emotions and needs of others.

The cup, linked to the element of Water and the zodiacal signs Cancer, Scorpio and Pisces, is also a sacred object in Christianity. The legend of the Holy Grail is still well known, the cup from which Christ drank during the Last Supper and with whom Joseph of Arimathea collected his blood. The cup is also one of the most common objects in daily life, as it is commonly used to hold liquids.

In the Tarot of Marseille, apart from the Ace and the Queen, all the cups are open.

The cards of the suit of Cups are the emotions of the heart: they express empathy and sentiment and can refer to acts of compassion. Having several in a spread means giving much importance to love and feelings.

ACE OF CUPS

The card is filled with a large cup, with the base consisting of three parts, a short stem decorated with three circles and a pattern similar to leaves. The upper part is reminiscent of a cathedral, with six lateral towers and a central façade decorated with various symbols depending on the deck, while from the base of the structure – in the central part of the cup – there are three decorations similar to the one on the base.

INTERPRETATION: This card is a chalice that can symbolize the hearth, the home, the family, a moment full of joy and leisure, reciprocated love, fun, pleasure, friendship. It can also refer to a period of abundance, fertility, fullness, beauty. It is the case of those who, for example, are starting a new emotional relationship and feel within themselves a sense of deep love, fullness, perfection. It can describe a phase in which everything seems to flow smoothly and we feel protected. **Or**: It can indicate a moment of frustration in our emotional life, sterility, sadness, inability to build a family; unrequited love, the impression that situations don't fit together the right way, the fear of committing to a relationship because of past disappointments.

KEYWORDS: Feeling, intuition, abundance, emotion, fulfilment, closure, instability.

MESSAGE: Love will return to you each time you offer it. Open your heart.

TWO OF CUPS

Two open cups are next to each other but separated by a decoration. From a horizontal base, occupying the lower part, begins a heraldic decoration that leads to a first flower at the height of the two cups. From the center of the flower starts another stem, which in turn branches into two fish-shaped decorations and a central motif, composed of a sort of open cup that culminates with a flower bud.

INTERPRETATION: The card represents the magnetic force that unites the opposites; it can describe falling in love, a chosen compatibility and reciprocated love, or wish for marriage, sincerity, friendship, deep affections and intense sexual activity. Love opens up to others and, in this way, can measure its own truth and intensity: this is true for relationships within a couple, but also in friendship or in the professional arena. Indeed, the card can also symbolize a fruitful agreement, a stable contract. Finally, it may symbolize a particularly charismatic and charming couple. **Or**: It can signal an unhappy union, infidelity, deception, betrayal, separation and obstacles in love. It can indicate the inability to open up to others due to selfishness or shyness; the need to feel deeply understood that is not currently fulfilled.

KEYWORDS: Union, attraction, a toast, friendship, collaboration, separation, dissatisfaction.

MESSAGE: Love lives when it is shared outside of ourselves.

THREE OF CUPS

Two cups are at the bottom while at the top, in the center, a third cup seems to be supported and wrapped by a decoration that branches off forming harmonious shapes. Overall, the effect of the decoration is to connect the three cups, taking the form of a fourth large cup and a heart.

INTERPRETATION: It can indicate expansion and a happy conclusion to a problem, relief, happiness for the birth of a child, abundance, joy of life. Even if the child is not yet born, it may indicate that, if we live in a relationship, we are ready for a pregnancy or to consolidate the union. It can also describe the enjoyment of something that has been created with love, personal balance, joy; the positive result of a compromise in which different interests have been reconciled to create a new situation that benefits everyone; a healing after a rather troubled period; a triumph in the professional sphere, especially if we work in show business or in the arts. **Or**: It can indicate false hopes, improbable projects and illusions in love, excess of pleasure, insincere affection, a crisis in a couple in which we cannot agree on how to make the relationship evolve; a physical attraction in which one lacks a true sense of closeness. Finally, it may represent a loss of prestige or an invitation to be more humble.

KEYWORDS: Joy, sharing, relief, prestige, superficiality, illusion.

MESSAGE: With the right company and solid foundations, success will come.

FOUR OF CUPS

The card represents four identical cups, separated vertically and horizontally by a floral decoration. At the center and at the upper end of the plant are two flowers separated by an extension of the plant, while the lower part ends with a flower emerging from a bud.

INTERPRETATION: The number Four is the symbol of stability and concreteness and expresses consolidation, which in the sentimental field can result in a stable relationship or a period without major changes that we wish to remain as such. In the professional field it may suggest that we have laid the foundations for a good business: a new company, or a project of which we can reap the rewards. It could refer to buying a home or acquiring something that provides us with emotional stability. **Or**: It can describe the apprehension that is felt despite an achieved success, or a crisis related to immobility; it is possible that we feel the desire to break the routine and expand our circle of knowledge, spicing up a stable relationship in which we risk getting bored; it can portray unexpected changes in love or in friendships. Finally, it may suggest caution with respect to people we have known for a short time: perhaps it's best to wait before trusting completely.

KEYWORDS: Emotional stability, concreteness, expectation, new friendships, routine, unexpected, caution.

MESSAGE: Safety is important, when it doesn't lead to inactivity.

FIVE OF CUPS

On the sides of the card are four cups, while a fifth is placed in the center, surrounded by a large floral decoration. Two bloomed flowers almost seem to embrace the central cup, enclosing it. The decoration then proceeds upward, opening into a flower which in turn contains a bud.

INTERPRETATION: It can represent an important change, especially on a sentimental level. At whatever point our relationship has arrived, we are ready to take another step forward; or there is a new element and thus we are ready for new relationships. It can also indicate that our love is reciprocated, that after a period of crisis it is time to reconcile. It may indicate a possible inheritance; an idea of love deeper than the feelings of a couple, that takes togetherness into account. It may indicate a kind and generous person, a point of reference for others. **Or**: A sense of discouragement, disillusionment because the progress we were expecting in our relationship is slow to come. Perhaps we want to be at the center of the world for someone, but we feel that it cannot be. Finally, we may tend to compulsively help others, with the silent intention of pleasing ourselves.

KEYWORDS: Evolution, sentimental change, reconciliation, legacy, generosity, disillusionment, sacrifice.

MESSAGE: Stability means taking risks, especially in love.

SIX OF CUPS

Six identical, parallel and perfectly aligned cups are divided by a complex decoration that develops vertically, composed of motifs in the shape of leaves and flowers. In the center, a flower with eight petals, while the top and bottom motifs are completely different from each other, in contrast with the perfect symmetry of the cups.

INTERPRETATION: The Six in the suit of Cups can represent a situation in which we feel satisfied, without great desire for change. It can indicate a relationship of a couple in which we tend toward positive symbiosis; the desire that everything remains as it is because we are living in a state of grace. It can express the pleasure of feeling part of a close-knit group, where we understand each other immediately. It can finally indicate a happy family life, in which communication flows smoothly and there is mutual respect. **Or**: We remain motionless out of fear, even if the situation requires change; we may remain in the nostalgic past, fearing that any interference might disturb our emotional balance, for example, by refusing to accept that our children have grown up. This attitude could prevent us from seeing problems, keeping us locked in our personal idea of how reality should be. This may apply to the relationship of a couple, friendships, or family relationships.

KEYWORDS: Nostalgia, pleasure, fulfillment, gift, understanding, closure, fixation.

MESSAGE: Don't think about the past, nor the future: live happiness now.

SEVEN OF CUPS

At the top and bottom of the card, the cups are arranged in two groups of three. In the center, the seventh cup is surrounded by a leaf decoration that starts from the central cup at the bottom and seems to form a further goblet, culminating around the central cup at the top.

INTERPRETATION: It may be that we are living an intense, passionate love, in which we want to protect the other, idealizing them even if it is not reciprocated. It can represent a romantic and idealistic person, who knows how to involve others in his projects. It can also indicate the enthusiasm and the will to contribute to the welfare of others, the tendency to want to help others. The arrival of someone or something that upsets the balance. **Or**: It may indicate an excessive need to feel accepted by others, leading us to want to always be the center of attention; the fear of revealing oneself due to lack of self-confidence. Finally, it can signal that we are deluding ourselves about our value, but without committing ourselves sufficiently (for example, we can feel important in our relationship, but we do nothing to nurture it).

KEYWORDS: Determination, passion, idealism, exclusivity, romance, exhibitionism, illusion.

MESSAGE: To remain in the spotlight you must be centered within yourself.

EIGHT OF CUPS

At the top and bottom the cups are arranged in two sets of three, as in the previous card. This time, however, at the center there are two cups, protagonists of the scene, and the decorative motif that surrounds them and separates them is perfectly symmetrical. In the center there is a flower with four petals, from which the entire decoration of flowers and leaves starts.

INTERPRETATION: It may indicate that we are seeking a complete balance, which unites material stability and emotional tranquility in ourselves and in our relationships. It is possible that we feel the need to consolidate friendships, a love, perhaps to settle ourselves in a new place to live (for example, buying furniture). It may refer to a period of profound reflection in which we feel that we deserve the best, a period that makes us feel centered, in harmony both family-wise and from an emotional and spiritual point of view. **Or**: The constant search for perfection can lead us to experience a sense of frustration and disappointment, due to the inability to always achieve a balanced and safe judgment. It is as if there were tensions between our aspirations and the current reality, which does not allow us to live serenely and in harmony. This can apply both to our inner self and to our relationships with others.

KEYWORDS: Determination, balance, idealism, exclusivity, perfectionism, frustration, illusion.

MESSAGE: Perfection is not of this world.

NINE OF CUPS

This time there are three groups of three, composed of perfectly symmetrical and identical cups. A pattern of leaves and flowers runs through the entire card both horizontally and vertically, surrounding the central cup.

INTERPRETATION: Nine being the number of wisdom, the card can indicate a period of progress and development in the emotional and relationship fields; the cups are arranged in a balanced and harmonious way and the central ones are surrounded by two branches, symbols of life, dynamism and fertility. The card can refer, for example, to a sense of balance from an emotional point of view, which provokes admiration; or to a period of psychophysical satisfaction and well-being. Finally, it can express our need to spread and share the goodness received. **Or**: Failure to evolve and to surpass our limits. This can generate a sense of inner disequilibrium, confusion with respect to what we really want; inability to feel satisfied with ourselves and our expectations of others. It is as if, despite having everything we need to be happy, we do not enjoy anything.

KEYWORDS: Satisfaction, well-being, satiety, pleasure, fulfillment, apathy, saturation.

MESSAGE: Be wise, you have everything you need to feel satisfied.

TEN OF CUPS

Three series of identical cups are arranged in a perfectly symmetrical way. At the top, a larger cup is placed horizontally. On it we see a small four–petaled flower. Apart from this detail, the card is very basic, with no flowers or leaves.

INTERPRETATION: In the card the largest cup could represent the profound joy that comes from having completed a commitment that allows us to distribute our contents to others. At this stage we are like a vessel of abundance: indeed, the card can indicate a happy person from an emotional point of view. It can suggest harmony, realization of projects and ambitions, reciprocated love, success, a house full of serenity and warmth. Being the last card, it may suggest that a cycle has just ended: we have reached the height of our fulfillment. Now we can wait for what will come from the universe. **Or**: It can indicate bitterness, misunderstanding, exploitation of others, inability to feel fully satisfied. It could call for greater generosity in relationships and in the family, because at this stage we may feel closed, unable to give something of ourselves to others.

KEYWORDS: Happiness, contentment, positive outcome, family harmony, happy moment, closure, misunderstanding.

MESSAGE: Giving means also making room to receive.

PENTACLES

They express a feminine energy, both passive and receptive like the Earth that contains and nourishes us. They describe our sense of security, also in relation to the things we possess and to feelings. Moreover, they symbolize the achievements and losses and what has value for us, the concrete commitment, a thorough study, biological research, geology. They are associated with the Earth element and with the signs Taurus, Virgo and Capricorn. It is the suit of traders, artisans, builders, workers, in general of all those who, for one reason or another, handle money and material instruments. Gold, of which the pentacle that represents this suit is made, is the noble metal par excellence. It is a symbol of abundance but it can also become a source of suffering, as in the legend of King Midas, condemned to turn anything into gold and, for this reason, deprived of the pleasure of living.

Unlike Swords and Wands, Pentacles are not identifiable with a weapon, nor do they have a specific function like the Cups. Their value is closely linked to the use made of them. Likewise, money can be a symbol of generosity or greed, of munificence or corruption.

The cards of the suit of Pentacles are the talents we possess: they express the income derived from our work and can refer to commercial trade. Having several in a spread means giving much importance to material aspects and also to one's financial status.

ACE OF PENTACLES

Although initially it appears to be a simple image, the Ace of Pentacles presents a very complex decoration, linked to the symbolism of the number 4. The card is dominated by a coin in the form of a large golden disc consisting of four circles at the center of which are three small fleur-de-lys, which can be found on every pentacle in the suit. The disc has branches and blossoms ending in a golden crown both at the top and bottom.

INTERPRETATION: It can represent what is tangible on the material level, that is, solid structures and what is obtained with money: employment contracts, good business, property, one's bank account. It describes a situation of euphoria, good news in the field of work or tied to a contract. A victory, a new business, a promotion, physical and mental energies that are spent to achieve stability in one's world. It can also refer to the physical body, suggesting that we are taking care of it and this makes us feel well. **Or**: Dependence on physical pleasure and material resources misused, attachment to things, avarice or excessive extravagance. It can also suggest that we are neglecting material aspects of life: money, one's body, physical pleasure.

KEYWORDS: Gain, materialism, acquisition, success, possession, matter, physicality.

MESSAGE: Something may bring you physical well being and economic stability.

TWO OF PENTACLES

A large band connects and encloses the two coins. Equally symmetrical leaves and flowers emerge from the band. Traditionally, in the two of Pentacles, are inserted the initials of the publisher. In this case, the edition was published by Lo Scarabeo in 2019. The acronym AMM.MO stands for the authors Anna Maria Morsucci and Mattia Ottolini.

INTERPRETATION: The card contains the symbol of infinity, created by the union of the two coins. It can indicate two sides of the same reality, inviting us to analyze the pros and cons of a situation. It can also describe a moment of great transformation, inevitably studded with doubts and perplexities; cycles of change, the need to make a choice: the indecision between two options that, in the same way, seem interesting to us. It can also indicate the union between two business partners, the choice between two businesses to be undertaken, the agreements linked to a contract. Finally, it may suggest that the achievement of a concrete result depends on how much the two parties are able to collaborate in view of a common goal. **Or**: It can indicate instability, contracts that do not go through, eternal indecision that makes us constantly oscillate between two professional or economic options, for example choosing whether to buy a new home or renovate that one you own and, through indecision, doing nothing.

KEYWORDS: Flexibility, inconstancy, society, rhythm, adaptability, indecision, hesitation.

MESSAGE: There is strength in unity, but beware of indecision.

THREE OF PENTACLES

Two coins at the bottom, both parallel and horizontal, seem to support a third, which occupies the upper half of the card. The floral decoration in the upper part seems to protect, highlighting the third coin and fortifying the base formed by the first two. The set of decorative shapes is harmonious and recalls two hearts.

INTERPRETATION: In the suit of Pentacles, the Three, number which indicates growth and success, represents the development and use of energy that leads to the creation of a concrete activity. The card can refer to business relations or to the start-up of a business, for example, a project for the construction of a house or the putting in writing of an operational plan for a new activity. It can also represent fame and success that come from commercial or work capability, or even from the use of one's own resources, physical prowess, artistic and manual skills that can bring money and economic growth. **Or**: It may indicate a failed business due to lack of planning, imprudent projects, inability to transform its resources into material successes. For example, it can describe the tendency to invest in bankrupt companies; the waste of money in unsafe investments. It can also indicate an aversion to risk that could clip our wings.

KEYWORDS: Planning, trade, talent, proceed by degrees, lack of skill, sloppiness.

MESSAGE: Success comes by transforming ideas into concrete achievements.

FOUR OF PENTACLES

We see four coins divided into two pairs. At the center there is a heraldic symbol with a rampant bull surmounted by a crown. Further floral decorations complement the card that looks extraordinarily rich and opulent.

INTERPRETATION: It is the number of stability and in the suit of Pentacles it is identified with what is real and concrete, such as a house or finances. Symbol of success, triumph, achievement. The card can indicate feeling lucky, a flourishing activity and the enjoyment of what has been achieved. It can also describe a period of economic and practical stability, financial successes. Finally, it can allude to a state of physical well-being: we are well and we feel beautiful. **Or**: It can describe an unstable phase linked to economic difficulties. It may also indicate that despite material well-being, we do not feel satisfied, because we are stuck on the practical aspects of existence. Excessive attention to material stability can make us lose sight of other things such as relationships or the pleasure of adventure. Finally, it may indicate that we do not feel fit.

KEYWORDS: Material stability, concreteness, possession, frugality, concentration, distrust, avarice.

MESSAGE: The goods you possess must not possess you.

FIVE OF PENTACLES

A coin at the center of the card is surrounded by four other coins, symmetrically arranged at the top and bottom. The composition is covered by colored leaves that completely surround the central coin, highlighting it and giving a sense of protection.

INTERPRETATION: The card may suggest that, if we can go beyond material stability, there is the possibility of producing something more original that will lead us to be protagonists like the central coin on the card. For example, while keeping earnings in mind, we can decide to undertake a job that is more in line with our true nature, assuming the risk of questioning our economic security; we can choose to treat our body well not for purely hedonistic purposes but for a specific goal, such as the practice of yoga, which can serve to reconcile the well-being of the body with that of the mind. **Or**: It can indicate an obstacle that upsets stability and well-being, a situation that suddenly arises and requires our attention, bringing us worries. For example, the arrival of a new employee at work, which requires time for training and caution to not disturb the existing balance.

KEYWORDS: Ambition, overcoming limits, new interests, search for balance to overcome stress, destabilization, discord, request for attention.

MESSAGE: Don't get ahead of yourself

SIX OF PENTACLES

There are six coins, divided into two groups of three by a cross-shaped blossom. This creates a mirror-like structure between the top and bottom sets, in which the two outer coins stand out, and seem to be protected by leaves. The card design is symmetrical.

INTERPRETATION: It could indicate a balance between desires and their practical realization. It can describe a phase of material and financial recovery; a charitable and generous person, able to help us, someone happy to share their riches with others, who displays love and openness toward his or her neighbor. Success in business and in material matters, aid, gifts and rewards. We can take pleasure from material life, perhaps because we feel satisfied with what we have, or because at this stage we tend to value our beauty and our well-being. **Or**: It can represent an imbalance linked to the inability to share equitably what one possesses, the tendency to dissipate money. It can indicate the propensity to trust the wrong people and get in debt; a mismatch between what we give and what we receive in return. Finally, it may concern a discrepancy between our work and the compensation we receive.

KEYWORDS: Generosity, favors, gift, balance between giving and receiving, equitable distribution, extravagance, bankruptcy.

MESSAGE: The management of resources requires balance and attention.

SEVEN OF PENTACLES

In the card we see four coins in the bottom half, two at the top and one at the center. From the lower part begins a decoration composed of leaves and flowers, which completely surrounds the central coin as if to protect it.

INTERPRETATION: If we know how to reconcile our practical skills and our creativity we can reach a tangible result in the material sphere. Concentration is needed: it is not always easy to harmonize security and ambition. At this time our activity may require special attention and caution. Like the center of a target, the central coin is an invitation to stay focused on the goal in order to achieve it. The card may also advise you to think carefully before acting. Only patience and commitment can ensure lasting success. **Or**: It may suggest that there is no balance between our projects and our practical sense; we may have very good ideas but do not know how to implement them, or are so practical that we cannot give up well-established habits and certainties. It can also indicate that we are 'playing it by ear' in the economic or work field, without a solid structure. This can make us feel disoriented.

KEYWORDS: Patience, commitment, focus, determination, balance between practicality and creativity, disorientation, dispersion.

MESSAGE: A house is built brick by brick, but with a clear plan of how to construct it.

EIGHT OF PENTACLES

There are eight coins arranged vertically in a perfectly symmetrical way. A decoration composed of a central flower with eight petals runs through them, from which another four flowers and four leaves branch off. Each coin is surrounded by a flower and a leaf.

INTERPRETATION: The number Eight in this suit can indicate balance on the material plane. It can also describe the ability to transform one's resources into concrete results, or symbolize rewards for the work done and easy earnings. It speaks of our ability to commit ourselves to improving our economic position. The result can come from a balanced management of our energies and the ability to network. Moreover, the card can refer to the idea that there is a balance between having and giving, so the rewards will be proportional to the effort we have made. Finally, it can indicate a routine in which we are immersed. **Or**: Frustration due to failure to achieve goals: either because we have given more than we received, or because we have not committed ourselves enough. It can warn of an imbalance in the management of our resources, including money.

KEYWORDS: Work, commitment, dedication, manual skills, employment, routine, imbalance.

MESSAGE: Just rewards are coming.

NINE OF PENTACLES

We find a central coin enclosed in a double decorative motif that culminates at the top and bottom into two flowers. The central coin symmetrically divides the rest of the card, with four coins above and four below, separated by a flower both up and down.

INTERPRETATION: The card may describe an evolution: having found balance, with the Eight card, between inner resources and materials, it is now possible to share what has been achieved with others and reap the fruits of our commitment. We can feel proud of what we have achieved, which gives us a profound sense of well-being and fulfillment. The Arcanum can indicate the achievement of the goals we have set ourselves, insurance, investment, prudence and savings, or an increase in capital due to a fortunate situation which allows us to grow. **Or**: The central coin can refer to a protected but solitary condition, in which we prefer to keep ourselves isolated and hidden, to prevent someone from taking away what we have painstakingly conquered. For example, it can refer to the fear that can be felt after a big win, for fear that someone will discover our new wealth.

KEYWORDS: Discernment, prudence, security, material serenity, sense of protection, luck, distrust, isolation.

MESSAGE: Resources produce joy if they are shared with others.

TEN OF PENTACLES

The ten coins are divided into two groups of five by a double central cross, which branches into leaves and flowers to compose a perfectly symmetrical decoration. Two coins are placed vertically up and down, and are crossed by the floral decoration that flows into two flowers.

INTERPRETATION: The card can describe a new creative cycle, the old one being finished. We have reached a high level of productivity which implies the overcoming of all that is physical, practical. The card can tell us about art and poetry: areas that typically produce money simply through their creative energy; a period of contentment and a happy lifestyle; concretization of energy and fullness. It can describe the awareness of having a lasting financial security, or profits, fortune, nobility and wealth deriving from a family inheritance. **Or**: It can indicate a sense of failure, economic well-being that does not give us satisfaction. It can also describe the risk of suffering losses or financial crises due to our inability to manage resources.

KEYWORDS: Fulfillment, family inheritance, sense of ethics, generosity, financial tranquility, waste of resources, sense of inadequacy.

MESSAGE: Rejoice in what you have, there is still so much to achieve.

CHAPTER FIVE

THE MINOR ARCANA: THE COURT FIGURES

The court figures of the Minor Arcana – Page, Knight, Queen and King – represent the people in our lives and sometimes some aspects of our personality. These cards describe, though in a less profound form, the forces that operate within us in different moments and spheres of existence: how we place ourselves in relation to a situation concerning work (Wands), intellectual aspects and rivals (Swords), affections (Cups) and material situations (Pentacles). With respect to the phases of life, the Pages indicate childhood and adolescence, the Knights youth and the early years of adulthood, while the Queens and the Kings indicate maturity.

The appearance of one of these figures in a spread of cards may represent ourselves or the people around us, and this we will understand by the context of the reading together with the other Arcana, Major or Numerical. If, for example, the reader wishes to have answers related to work, he can evaluate a card that represents him among the Court Figures of the suit of Wands, taking into account his age, the role he currently holds and his future objectives. He will therefore either be a novice apprentice (Page), a person in search of advancement (Knight), a female figure who exercises power (Queen) or a male character who holds the highest authority (King). Obviously, the same applies to the other suits for their areas of reference.

DESCRIPTION OF THE COURT FIGURES

The sixteen Court Figures of the Minor Arcana are described in detail below. Each description is divided into the following sections:

Interpretation: Where the main meanings of the Arcanum are analyzed.

Question: It has the task of stimulating our intuition through visualization and active imagination.

Keywords: Where the fundamental terms that outline the card are indicated.

Message of the Court Card: An indication that may be useful as a response to a question.

PAGE OF WANDS

A young man in profile seems to be advancing toward our right. With both hands he holds a large staff with cut branches, almost as tall as he is, wider at the bottom and narrower at the top; he wears a hat with flowing hair, and a short suit, covered with a cape, open on his back. The scene takes place outdoors, as seen from the ground and two plants at the bottom.

INTERPRETATION: The page is facing with his whole body toward our right, that is, the future. Pages represent the beginning of a journey. In the suit of Wands, this beginning can be characterized by enthusiasm and spirit of adventure. It can symbolize a young collaborator, an apprentice or it may concern the beginning of a relationship that could result in a physical encounter, a new work activity that requires energy, vitality, commitment. In general, it can signal that something new is about to start and can take on a concrete, stable form, like a wand. It can also indicate the determination and the desire to take risks to experience change. Finally, it can advise not to use our own creative energy to hurt others, but to support ourselves: in fact, the stick is not lifted but used as a support. **Or**: It could symbolize indecision, lack of vitality, a period in which we feel unenthusiastic. It can also warn us about the tendency to be unfocuased or incapable of having goals, objectives, a direction in which to look. Finally, it can signal a period of stagnation, in which we fail to realize anything, or in which we do not find something valid that could stimulate or interest us.

QUESTION: Who or what is the young man looking at?

KEYWORDS: Vitality, creativity, new business, new passion, enthusiasm, fear, tendency to postpone.

MESSAGE: Be enthusiastic and focused, use your energy.

KNIGHT OF WANDS

A knight on his steed seems to look carefully at the stick which he holds with one hand. He wears a broad-brimmed hat, from which thick hair emerges, while his horse is covered by a broadcloth below which two hooves can be seen. Both Knight and horse have their bodies turned toward our left and their gaze directed toward the opposite direction. As a background, below you can see the ground and a tuft of grass.

CAVALIER DE BATON

INTERPRETATION: While the page held his staff without considering it, the knight is looking directly at it. His body turned to our left and his gaze toward our right can make us think of a transition phase, in which we feel called to act according to values and habits that we learned over time, but our mind is elsewhere, aimed at goals closer to our feelings. For example, it may concern the decision process that leads to a career in a completely new field, while we are still doing another job. It may also suggest that, although a part of us is clinging to past issues, we are becoming aware of our creative resources or our power. Finally, it may concern a journey or a relocation for work reasons. **Or**: It may refer to an inability to imagine the future and perceive our resources. Given that the stick can also be a weapon meant to harm, we might think of a young person who is impulsive, irascible, who acts aggressively. Finally, it may refer to the disorientation that arises when one is suspended between the need to please others and the need to follow one's instincts.

QUESTION: How will he use the stick?

KEYWORDS: Determination, passage, exploration, decision, reflection, disorientation, aggression.

MESSAGE: Think big, act in an informed and conscious way.

QUEEN OF WANDS

A queen with long hair looks toward our right. She is seated, though not necessarily on a throne; the back of a seat is visible behind the crook of her arm. On her shoulder rests a large staff that the queen clasps to her without looking at it. The waves of her hair, the position of the arms and her posture make her seem to be moving. The arms flow toward the knees, as if she were about to get up. A hand holds a piece of cloth that covers the dress at the height of her legs.

REYNE DE BATON

INTERPRETATION: The suit of Wands, directed at the feminine, loses the aggressiveness and masculine impetuosity, becoming dynamic and flexible. The position of the Queen seems to refer to a phase of gathering energy. Long, flowing hair suggests vitality. The card can symbolize an enterprising and determined person; a passionate temperament, proud and attention-seeking. It can describe a phase of enthusiasm, desire to live and act, the certainty of having the energy necessary to achieve a project. It can represent a woman in her proactive way of relating to work; a colleague, a strong and determined manager, or even a man who expresses his creativity in a considered, almost feminine manner. **Or**: It can indicate distrust, a phase in which we feel threatened and keep the stick close to defend ourselves. It can represent a person who is not very energetic or too controlled; a desire to live brought to excess resulting in the continuous search for pleasures and gratifications; presenting oneself too cautiously and with excessive self-reflection. Finally, it may indicate coldness or lack of enthusiasm.

QUESTION: What will her next action be?

KEYWORDS: Vitality, energy, dynamism, seductive power, magnetism, mistrust, fickleness.

MESSAGE: Your instincts and your energy are your best weapons.

KING OF WANDS

A young king grasps in one hand a large stick that acts as a scepter, while the other hand is on his corresponding leg at the height of his belt. He seems to be leaning rather than sitting on the throne, the position of the left leg seems to indicate that he is ready to get up or sit down. His body and his gaze are turned toward our right, a foot pointing to our left. He is dressed in a finely decorated suit and his crown is surrounded by a broad hat with a wide and stiff brim.

INTERPRETATION: The big hat, the stick and the hand at the height of the king's belt refer to an energy that can attain success, balancing instinct and reason; it can also represent a strong, confident and passionate person who, thanks to his determination, fulfills a role of responsibility: a leader, an entrepreneur; someone who has made through his own creative talent his own 'kingdom': an actor or an intellectual. It could even be a charismatic man who is committed to serving society. The large hat surrounding the crown may refer to power used wisely. It can indicate that the resources and energy to achieve success are there, along with the maturity necessary to manage it in the best possible way. **Or**: It could indicate an excess of impulsivity or rationality: one risks acting inappropriately or not acting; a person who holds a leadership role without being able to, for example, to show an enthusiasm not supported by adequate skills. It can symbolize excessive or insufficient self-confidence or a presumptuous person: someone who is "all smoke and no fire".

QUESTION: How did he direct his energy to get where he is?

KEYWORDS: Security, entrepreneur, boss, commitment, experience, initiative, presumption, incapacity.

MESSAGE: Power must be handled with care knowing that nothing lasts forever.

PAGE OF SWORDS

A young man looks toward our left; he wears a large hat and a cape that seems to move in the air. In one hand he grasps the scabbard, while in the other he holds a sword in a rather unnatural way. His feet are open and well planted on the ground, and in the background below the presence of vegetation leads us to think that he is outdoors. There is a contrast between the front-facing posture and his gaze – to one side – and his feet which point in opposite directions.

INTERPRETATION: The posture, the direction of his gaze and the way in which the page holds his sword, may refer to the idea of an insecure person, who does not know whether to act or to wait. It can represent an inexperienced person, who underestimates his ideas. He may be a young apprentice who prefers to speak little so as not to feel embarrassed among more experienced people; a young university researcher, a student. The card may suggest caution and advise us to take time before speaking, continue to pursue our interests further; a young person, a child, perhaps an adolescent who is building his own vision of the world; someone who, even if somewhat older, maintains the attitude of an adolescent: the classic Peter Pan. **Or**: It could describe a character who continues to feel insecure, despite having reached the maturity of thought necessary to express their opinion; a person who digs in their heels, focused on an idea without solid foundations: a youth who speaks inappropriately, showing excessive self-confidence not supported by adequate preparation. Finally it can refer to fruitless chitchat, useless discussions.

QUESTION: How will he use his sword?

KEYWORDS: Apprenticeship, inexperience, child, adolescence, reflection, indecision, ramblings.

MESSAGE: Keep your feet on the ground.

KNIGHT OF SWORDS

A knight dressed in armor with a conspicuous mask on the shoulder of the same arm with which he holds his sword. The horse has a stiff armor and his front legs are raised off the ground. The two main characters – the horse and the rider – are facing to our left. The scene takes place outside, as shown by the landscape in which some plants are present.

INTERPRETATION: The direction of the characters (horse and knight) toward our left can refer to a phase of transition between past and present; a thought that is not based on the certainty of our ideas, but on fidelity to one's role, based on convictions and rules imposed from the outside. The card may describe an enterprising and courageous person, of noble spirit, reliable and capable of defending the values in which he believes, even at the cost of putting himself aside; a person who challenges himself and others; a young but influential man, with enforceable powers: a military man, a policeman, a lawyer, someone capable of using drastic means, to defend the law or a cause in which he believes. It can also indicate grit, impetuousness, fight against injustice. Finally, it may concern a trip or a relocation for intellectual or legal reasons. **Or**: It can describe a fierce adversary, a rival with whom we must fight; a person animated by false ideals or incapable of acting and defending what he believes. It can be someone who abuses his role, a bully, a crook, a cynical and unscrupulous person. The card can also indicate that we are tired of obeying the rules and we want to start thinking with our own head.

QUESTION: For whom or what is he fighting?

KEYWORDS: Incisiveness, courage, warrior, impetus, value, law, hostility.

MESSAGE: Make sure your actions match your values and your thoughts.

QUEEN OF SWORDS

A queen, facing our left, sits on the throne. In one hand she wields a sword while the other rests on her belly, which appears pregnant: a detail underlined by the rich drapery of her dress which forms an oval. The woman is dressed in a sober and elegant manner and wears a collar with eight decorative stitches, the number referring to Arcanum VIII (Justice). Her head is surrounded by a crown and her hair is loose.

INTERPRETATION: The sitting position and posture of the queen facing our left refer to an introspection tied to the past and a passive attitude. The image makes one think of an intelligent person, independent and with great intellectual capabilities, who in their life has often found themselves having to fight to defend their own ideas. She could be a single woman, a widow or a separated woman, who favors her own convictions and respect for rules. It can also describe a wise woman, capable of putting her ideas into practice, effective, able to defend her values with pride. It could be a figure of power, with a role of responsibility in public administration, in the military or legal field (a policewoman, a lawyer, a judge, a politician) or perhaps in the intellectual sphere (a teacher or university professor). **Or**: It can describe a rival from an emotional point of view, a person suffering from loneliness or a hard, cruel and sly woman. If carried to excess, the tendency to intellectualize and the constant search for ideals to defend can turn into obstinacy and an excess of rationality, with a consequent rejection of the body and sexuality.

QUESTION: How will she deal with her condition?

KEYWORDS: Honesty, decision, wisdom, strength, implacability, loneliness, rudeness.

MESSAGE: Learning to compare yourself to others sharpens your wisdom.

KING OF SWORDS

A king, seated on a large, square-shaped stool, holding a sword in one hand and a scepter in the other. The scepter is pointing downwards. He is wearing elaborate armor: there is a mask on each shoulder. He has a wide-brimmed hat, above which there is a crown. His pose is unusual: his head is turned toward our right, his torso faces front, while his legs and feet are turned toward our left. His posture appears vigilant more than stable.

INTERPRETATION: The king may describe a person with an aptitude for commanding, for example a judge, a high-ranking military person, a doctor who is a department head. With his ability to handle blades, it may also refer to a surgeon. In any case, it is a person with a spirit of initiative, dynamic, engaged in a position of power that is to be exercised with care and defended against possible attacks; a personality of intellectual importance, well-regarded in society (an enlightened leader, a university professor, a jurist, a philosopher) who knows how to control his own thoughts and put them to good use in the world. **Or**: It can refer to an arrogant, dishonest figure, overly attached to his ideas, willing to resort to any means to impose them. It can also indicate a rival who holds positions of power or suggest that we feel insecure in our abilities and authority: for example, we occupy an important role, yet are incapable of asserting our ideas. Finally, it may refer to a person who, despite being older, has not had the opportunity to learn and thus feels insecure in his knowledge and his way of expressing himself.

QUESTION: How does he feel in his position?

KEYWORDS: Judge, power, authority, charisma, order, arrogance, dishonesty.

MESSAGE: Wisdom, culture and experience are not weapons but gifts to be shared.

PAGE OF CUPS

A young man in loose clothing seems to be walking on land strewn with small plants. He is looking toward a large open cup that he supports in one hand, while holding the lid in the other...but it could also be his hat. The cup is partially covered by a piece of cloth that seems to be part of his clothing. His head is uncovered and surrounded by a floral wreath.

INTERPRETATION: The page depicted in the card is turned toward our left and seems focused on the cup that is linked to the element of water, emotions, feelings, but also the deepest part of ourselves. His clothing and posture indicate sweetness, delicacy, passivity. The card can represent a young and inexperienced person, undecided on whether to declare his feelings or keep them to himself, perhaps a very sensitive and generous young man; it may suggest a certain shyness and the need to protect one's inner sphere, keeping it partially hidden. It can describe the initial phase of a relationship in which we don't know whether to show our feelings or repress them; the need to heal past wounds before falling in love again. A young man we love, such as a son, nephew or younger brother. **Or**: It could symbolize an immature person, undecided, or tied up in the past and unable to experience new relationships. It can also indicate a cold, insensitive character, who has become cynical through suffering; someone who moves from one flirtation to the next without ever committing, remaining in a constant state of being in love: a person "in love with love", but unable to become attached.

QUESTION: Who or what can make him open or close the cup?

KEYWORDS: Messenger, youth, initial enthusiasm, curiosity, falling in love, superficiality, inexperience.

MESSAGE: Don't waste the contents of your cup.

KNIGHT OF CUPS

A knight holds the bridle with one hand. With the other one he supports a large open cup which he is focused on. The horse is holding up his front paw corresponding to the hand with which the knight holds the cup. The man's head is uncovered, his hair loose, and his clothing is simple. The scene takes place outdoors, the ground appears somewhat bumpy but this does not seem to bother him.

INTERPRETATION: The figure on horseback proceeds toward our left, indicating the past and our receptive side. He may be bringing a gift, perhaps his own heart, expressing his feelings. The card can represent generous love, a person capable of great emotional impulses, not moderated by rationality (the rider does not protect himself with a helmet or armor). It can also symbolize someone who can give up their own security, giving of himself to others. The animal (which could be his instinctive side) moves in tune with him: the balance between instinct and emotions. Furthermore, it can symbolize a reconciliation and the ability to forgive. It can indicate a simple, young, spontaneous person who does not need to shield himself behind appearances: an artist, ready for success; a lover who gives of himself without reserve. Finally, it may concern a journey or a relocation for reasons of the heart. **Or**: It could indicate a selfish or overly generous person; someone who tends to make commitments and to say yes even when he should say no; a hypocritical person who pretends to be modest, or someone who is unable to forgive. It could describe a difficulty in managing emotions. Finally, a seducer, someone able to flatter us with his attentions but of whom we should be wary.

QUESTION: Where is he taking the Cup?

KEYWORDS: Seducer, generosity, goodness, balance, reward, selfishness, flattery.

MESSAGE: Do not be afraid to give of yourself.

QUEEN OF CUPS

A queen is seated. Behind her is a canopy that seems to protect her head. She is wearing a hat with a crown on top of it and elegant clothing. Her hair is long and loose. With one hand she wields a large closed cup spherical in shape, while in the other she holds a scepter that rests on her shoulder. Both the cup and the scepter seem to be supported on her legs.

INTERPRETATION: The queen looks toward our left: the past and the emotional, receptive side. The cup is closed: its content is protected. It could contain something precious that we wish to keep for those closest to us, for example, our love or our best qualities. It can represent a woman in love who puts feelings and family first. The shape of the closed cup is spherical and refers to the idea of perfection. It can indicate a wise person who sees beyond appearances: a psychotherapist, someone who is able to observe reality in its entirety. It can represent a woman who guards her own and others' feelings, and to whom we can confide our secrets. The scepter could refer to the ability to defend the contents of the cup or express the power that the Queen exercises over others. For a man it can indicate the woman loved, who exerts an influence on him. Finally, it can describe a person who has a gift recognized by others, for example an artistic gift. **Or**: It can represent a woman who does not let herself go to her feelings, one who is closed and does not show her talents or emotions. It can also indicate a superficial person, too attentive to appearances, who cannot reveal herself authentically.

QUESTION: What does the closed cup contain?

KEYWORDS: Love, protection, woman in love, artist, intuition, closure, superficiality.

MESSAGE: You have a precious gift: take care of it.

KING OF CUPS

A bearded King is seated on a low-backed throne. With one hand he wields an open cup, while the other is resting on the side at the height of his belt. He is wearing a large hat and a crown. His hair is covered by a sort of ear flap. His head and gaze are turned toward our right, in the opposite direction of the cup. His bust faces front and his legs are turned toward our left.

INTERPRETATION: The king looks toward our right, without focusing on the cup: he can represent a mature and successful individual who wants to direct his feelings toward new perspectives. It can indicate the man one loves or one's own willingness to fall in love. It can also symbolize a wise and authoritative person who has achieved inner balance and is able to help others overcome their turmoil. A father or strong figure of reference from an emotional point of view. He could be a doctor, a psychotherapist, a religious person, an artist or a patron, a wise friend to turn to for advice and comfort. His clothing is not opulent, indicating that appearances are of little interest to him. The large hat, combined with the crown, may reflect his ability to not yield to easy sentimentality; he knows how to mediate between the rational and the instinctive, as the hand resting on his belt also seems to emphasize. **Or**: It can indicate a person who does not pay attention to feelings, who lets himself be carried away by impulse or remains closed in his rationality. It can be a selfish or narcissistic man, overly focused on himself; a father, a strong figure of reference, by whom we do not feel loved, listened to, nor protected.

QUESTION: Why is he looking away from the cup?

KEYWORDS: Charisma, composure, patron, sage, advice, coldness, detachment.

MESSAGE: Be the master of your emotions.

PAGE OF PENTACLES

A young man wears a broad-brimmed hat that hangs to one side and holds in one hand a large coin which he looks at intensely, while with the other hand he touches his belt. On the ground one sees another coin corresponding to the one above it. His bust faces front, while the feet are open and point in opposite directions. The scene takes place outdoors; on the ground we can see some plants.

INTERPRETATION: The page looks to our left and is focused on the coin above. It may indicate an occasion which we chance upon that brings us something new in the work or financial field. For example, an unexpected task, or a small payout. It can also describe a phase in which we pay more attention to the economic side of things, perhaps saving, in view of a goal to be achieved: the purchase of a car, a computer or jewelry, but nothing too demanding. The coin on the ground may indicate that we have not yet depleted our reserves; it could be an invitation to exploit external resources that seem more obvious, for example, a contact that could prove useful for a career, or allows us to highlight our qualities. It could describe a teenager who is learning to manage money independently. **Or**: It could represent a person who pays too much attention to money, who is stingy, unwilling to invest or, on the contrary, excessively lavish; a limited vision of things, that prevents us from seizing opportunities and taking full advantage of our resources. Finally, it may suggest that we are too focused on a single aspect of reality and this prevents us from progressing.

QUESTION: Why is there a coin on the ground?

KEYWORDS: Practicality, economics student, attention to money, exploitation of resources, financial balance.

MESSAGE: Discover your hidden resources.

KNIGHT OF PENTACLES

A figure on horseback wears a hat with hair sticking out of it. He holds a stick and goes along with his horse toward our right. An arm and leg are not visible, while the horse has a raised front leg as if it were moving. A coin appears like a sun at the top right in the background. On the ground, the landscape is dotted with small plants.

INTERPRETATION: The rider faces our right which is the future, and seems to be guided by the coin, which looks similar to a sun, as if to indicate that it is his guide. The stick, which he holds and rests on his shoulder, can be a sign of great creative energy and will to make things happen. The card can indicate an ambitious person, willing to resort to drastic means (the stick) in order to achieve his objectives. The coin, in the form of the Sun, can also represent a higher plan, a task, or a real mission that must be accomplished. It can symbolize an instinctive and practical person, dynamic and courageous in his choices, able to think big; a rising entrepreneur, a trader, a financial consultant, a person able to make money thanks to his business skills, for example an artist or craftsman, a representative or a courier. Finally, it may concern a trip or relocation for economic reasons. **Or**: It can represent an aggressive person who is guided solely by the "money god"; someone who throws himself into investments without criteria. It can also indicate pettiness or opportunism; a tendency to not want to grow economically to avoid risks or to not have to fight.

QUESTION: Where does the money lead him?

KEYWORDS: Realism, professionalism, service, ambition, seriousness, pragmatism.

MESSAGE: There exists more than just the "money god".

QUEEN OF PENTACLES

REYNE DE DENIERS

A queen is completely in profile, facing our left and staring at the coin that she hold up in her hand, while in the other hand she holds a scepter. Her hair is gathered under her crown. It appears from her dress that a leg is stretched forward, as if she were in the act of standing up or stepping forward. She is the only Queen represented completely in profile.

INTERPRETATION: The queen looks at her coin, turned toward our left. It can describe a person who must manage an ongoing activity – for example a shop or a family business – or administer an inheritance. In general, it can represent a pragmatic woman, careful with money, practical and able to use her own resources; an assiduous worker who enjoys the comforts and security that money provides; a person who cares about their well-being and who takes care of their image by dressing in a refined manner. It may suggest the attitude to increase one's income, thanks to concentration and commitment. The scepter with a flower motif on top can represent our seductive power to obtain material goods: it can be a person who married for profit, perhaps someone who obtained a prestigious job thanks to their own attractiveness. **Or**: It can represent a stingy or materialistic person, whose only goal is money, or who spends too much to show off a wealth they do not have in reality; someone who is not able to manage their finances or to take care of their body. Finally, it can refer to the inability to look to the future and cultivate pleasant interests: everything must have only an economic purpose.

QUESTION: What will she do with the coin?

KEYWORDS: Safekeeping, heiress, wealth, protection, conservation, jealousy, avarice.

MESSAGE: Money is neither good nor bad. Our way of using it is good or bad.

KING OF PENTACLES

A mature bearded man with a wide hat sits cross-legged in a position that seems tangled. The upper body is tuned in the direction of his gaze, toward our right, the torso and legs are oriented to our left. His clothing and accessories are simple, as is the chair on which he is seated. He has no crown nor scepter. He holds a coin in one hand while the other rests at his side.

INTERPRETATION: The king is the emblem of power and, in the Pentacles, becomes a symbol of authority in the material world. It can describe a wise man who values stability and economic security, who knows how to manage his assets with prudence and foresight because he is already satisfied with what he has obtained; an experienced merchant who enjoys the fruits of his labors; a person with great practical sense: a banker, a builder, a wealthy entrepreneur or an economist; a person who knows the value of money because in order to succeed he counted only on his strength. The absence of regal attributes can symbolize that his power is practical, not abstract, and that money does not help him to show off his social position: it is a starting point to look beyond, remaining calm in his place; a person able to sniff out investments and seize opportunities on the fly. **Or**: It can indicate an immature or not very stable person from a financial point of view; someone who invests his money in a rash way; an individual who has not been able to grasp opportunities due to distrust or fear. Finally, someone who uses money to blackmail or bribe others.

QUESTION: Why is he sitting outdoors?

KEYWORDS: Administration, merchant, practical intelligence, a nose for business, success, greed, imprudence.

MESSAGE: Enjoy what you have, looking toward the future.

CHAPTER SIX

GUIDELINES FOR INTERPRETATION

Now that the cards have been analyzed in detail, we have arrived at our journey's destination. The way of the Tarot has been marked, yet questions still remain. Some of these are rather urgent: how do I memorize all the meanings of each card? How can I use all this information to read a spread of cards? How do I choose, among all this variety of meanings, the right one?

Abandon all the old beliefs or the ideas that have been instilled through years of superficial readings or "sellers of fear" that, when reading the cards, predict misfortune or the arrival of unavoidable disasters. The Tarot is not this. As you have seen, it is much more, and at the same time much less, because they can be precious instruments of introspection and investigation but also a real button to create self-fulfilling prophecies. For better or for worse.

Having said that, no special predisposition is needed to learn how to read the Tarot, if not the desire to apply and listen to our intuition. It is not true that it takes 'fluency', that the cards are 'inherited' (or similar things). To be able to read the Tarot does not require a great effort of memory, just let yourself be guided by the images for the Major Arcana and the construction of the card for the Minor Arcana, taking into account the significance of the number and symbols that are represented.

APPROACHING THE DECK

Try taking the deck of 22 Major Arcana in your hand and draw the cards; start looking at them one by one and let the evocative power of the images guide you. When you look at a card, analyze the emotions it conveys to you, try to associate it with a situation you've been through, something that has happened to you or to someone you know, a state of mind you've been in. This is a way to start memorizing the symbols and relate to their meanings via free associations. You can approach the Minor Arcana in much the same way, looking at them together at first, then one by one. As for the numerical cards, look at the whole sequence of ten cards: the way in which the suits are grouped together within the single Arcana so as to see how the numbers are constructed (for example 4+4+1=9), to see if there are flowers or leaves, if the decoration highlights a certain suit. This will help you come into closer contact with the meanings and befriend them. Through visualization and practice (it is very important to try and try again) you will be able to master the meaning of the cards in a short period of time.

To establish a rapport with the Arcana, absorbing their symbolism and their imagery, we propose a method that we often use during our seminars: we draw a card from the 22 Major Arcana, we place it in front of us, we observe it and answer the following questions:

- *What do I like about this card, and what inspires hostility and resistance instead?*
- *How does it resemble me? To what extent do I feel similar to this person/situation in life? On the other hand, how much do I differ from it?*
- *Which are the more benevolent and more critical meanings that I can attribute to this card?*
- *In which situation would I choose this card as my guide?*
- *Which of my acquaintances would I give this card to?*

The considerations that come up will tell us something about ourselves and about our relationships. Something that one can perceive as more or less useful and important but that is indubitably an opportunity to reflect, get to know oneself better, connect to one's emotions and reawaken one's creativity, which is often weakened by our daily routine. By handling the cards, which is to say interacting with them, you begin to transfer energy to the deck (which you have not inherited or found, which hasn't fallen from the skies: you have chosen it!). A result which some strengthen through rituals. The choice of the ritual is entirely personal: in any case, keeping the cards in a special cloth or a precious box reflects the respect and the value that they have for us. Only do it if it gives you a positive feeling; what matters is that you come to a harmony with the cards. The ritual is a means, not an end, its purpose is merely to put you in the right headspace. Don't feel obliged to do it. What's essential is that you find the right method for you.

CURIOSITY: Some advise using crystals to make the deck even more sensitive: heliotrope for foresight, lapis lazuli which influences the psyche, agate to combat anxiety, tiger's eye which indicates success and willpower. As it occurs with crystals, it is advisable to expose your cards to the full moon, to charge the deck with positive energy.

The consultation must occur only when you feel ready, when a rapport has been established between you and the deck; when handling it you feel that it is in harmony with your person. Don't be afraid to start the consultation and say the first thing that comes to mind. Experience shows that this is often the right one. **The more you think rationally, the greater the risk of losing the true message of that Arcanum.**

APPROACHING THE QUESTIONER

After getting acquainted with the deck, it's fundamental to learn how to listen to whomever asks for a reading. This does not only mean listening attentively to their story their questions and their expectations, but also observing them, picking up on non-verbal language (how they move, how they gesticulate, their gaze, their posture in the chair, etc.) which often says more than words. When interacting with them you must be sympathetic and respectful, never imposing your own view or ideas. By asking you for a consultation they are opening the doors to their heart, or at the very least they are telling you a part of themselves. It's up to you to approach their world on tiptoe, without purporting to know the truth, even after having gathered experience. We are never to feel like "illuminated masters", nor to present the questioner with information as if it were absolute truth. The Tarot allows us to gain a perspective on a situation but its responses are not set in stone and it does not have all the answers. If the scene described by the cards isn't a welcome one, or if they do not correspond to the questioner, accept their point of view and don't impose your own. Remember that symbols hold more than one meaning and the interpretation you give is always filtered by your mental structures and your projections.

HOW TO PROCEED IN THE READING

Before starting, shuffle the cards well. You may do it yourself or let the questioner do it. In either case, ask them to cut the deck and ask a question. The cut should be done preferably with their left hand, which is connected to their emotions, intuition and instinct. Before offering the deck to the questioner, make sure the deck is shuffled well. After it's been cut, put it back together and look at the two cards of the cut which often already give important information regarding what their state of mind is during the reading and whether their question actually hides a whole other topic.

Using the Tarot is like receiving the opinion of a wise friend who can help us gain a new perspective, which is why it's best to have a question to ask. The more detailed it is, the easier it is to receive an answer that can be taken as advice. It is best to avoid questions whose answer is a simple yes or no, as well as overly generic questions. It is best to ask open questions, such as: how can I best overcome this issue?

When you draw a card, consider its various meanings attentively, and only later decide which could be the most relevant in that particular situation. Allow your intuition to guide you, without being conditioned. **Following the Tarot's suggestions blindly is the antithesis of what they truly represent**, a tool that allows us to gain a greater awareness of ourselves and of the period we're going through.

WARNING: If the cards do not seem to be responding, stop. Let a few days pass (at least a week), and then, perhaps, try asking the same question. It's useless to get fixated and ask the same things obsessively.

PRELUDE TO THE READING

Some card reading systems are best for general issues, whereas others are more suitable for getting answers to specific questions.

It's fundamental to think and interpret the Arcana in a mindset of growth and development of the person. Even when it is a matter of making "pre-visions", envision the range of obstacles and opportunities that could come to pass, bearing in mind that interpreting the Tarot means familiarizing oneself with symbolic meanings. That said, prudence and common sense are essential to the interpretations formed for oneself and for others, because often people are afraid of what the future holds for them and it is also too easy to generate a feeling of mistrust, or to exaggerate when it comes to creating expectations.

READING TAROT FOR ONESELF

Reading Tarot on one's own is a very enriching but also rather risky experience. It's a sort of meditation which, with the right experience, can become a constructive act which allows us to analyze ourselves in relation to the various aspects of our lives. In case you wish for divinatory answers, be very careful: without the mediation of an external eye there's a great risk of seeing all the worst (or all the best) of what you've asked to see. If you are too much inside the issue, it's hard to look at it with a certain detachment. A trick to overcome this is to accept that the cards come out as a piece of advice. A very simple strategy is that of using the card (or the cards) in various aspects of your life that exclude consultation. For example: using a card that struck you in a particular way as the background on your phone, or as the bookmark for the book you're reading (or textbook you're studying). Make it part of your everyday life. By assimilating it you make it yours and understand its meaning, without thinking necessarily about a certain response. In this way you will reach a harmony with the message that the Arcanum holds for you, and perhaps held from the very beginning without you realizing it. In case you fear the response to a certain question, you can use another very efficient strategy: looking at the cards faceup, knowingly pick one or more Arcana that represent the answer you're looking for. The images of the Arcana will thus become a sort of amulet, a good luck charm, which will accompany you in your search and in the achievement of your goal.

READING METHODS

THE CARD OF THE DAY

It is a reading that can be done alone. In the morning or in the evening, without asking any particular question, the questioner draws a single card. In this way the Arcanum will also be a source of inspiration on how to best face the day.

THE GYPSY METHOD

It's a very simple system, to be used when you wish for a response to a specific question.

Use the 22 Major Arcana and draw three, to be arranged horizontally.

Where I'm coming from | *Current situation* | *Future outlooks*

THE TWO OPTIONS

A variation of the Gypsy method to be used when you are at a crossroads. It entails a binary spread to answer a specific question clearly. Place a single card above, face up, to indicate the questioner's situation (example: which is better, this job or that job?). Now, place two rows of three cards in a cascade arrangement on the left and right of this card; each row is to be interpreted with the Gypsy method (see image above). By comparing the two readings it will be possible to choose which of the two options is best.

DIRECT QUESTION METHOD

This is one of the most used card reading methods. It is simple and allows for an excellent vision of the greater picture of the questioner's situation. You can use the whole deck or just the 22 Major Arcana.

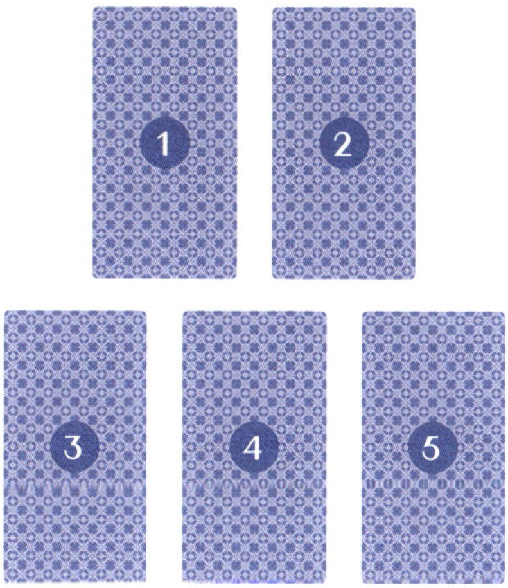

- **Card 1 (in favor):** Summarizes the circumstances working in the questioner's favor
- **Card 2 (against):** Describes the unfavorable circumstances
- **Card 3 (current situation):** General situation
- **Card 4 (final result):** The sentence that will provide the answer
- **Card 5 (advice):** The advice for facing the answer

This reading method is for answering a concrete question and understanding the developments of an issue. After shuffling and cutting the deck, arrange the cards from left to right.

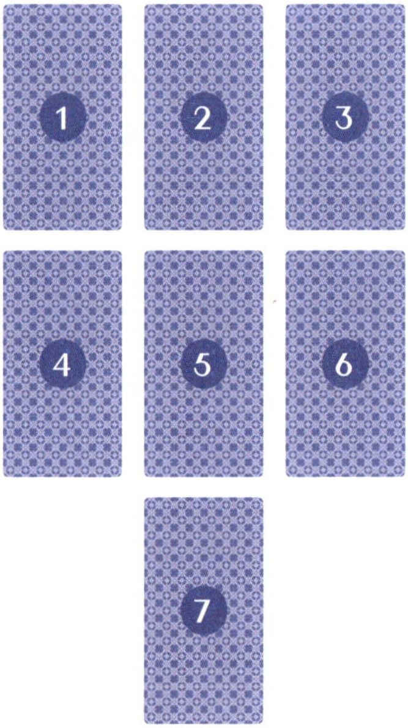

- **Card 1 (past situation):** Facts that may have influenced the situation you're examining
- **Card 2 (present situation):** Facts that are influencing the questioner
- **Card 3 (future outlooks):** Provides a first response to the questioner's question
- **Card 4 (line of conduct):** How the questioner should act to make their desires come true
- **Card 5 (close people)**: The actions of others, which can be favorable or unfavorable to the questioner
- **Card 6 (obstacles)**: Obstacles that one must overcome to solve the problem
- **Card 7 (final result)**: Future consequences of the answer the card has given

THE ASTROLOGICAL METHOD

The astrological spread is very useful for a general reading that allows you to analyze different aspects of life. The meaning of the 12 categories is similar to that of the horoscope's 12 astrological houses. The spread can be read in two ways: as a view of the big picture or as a guide for the year, the first card indicating the current month, the second the following and so on. After shuffling and cutting the deck, arrange the 12 carts in a circle counter-clockwise.

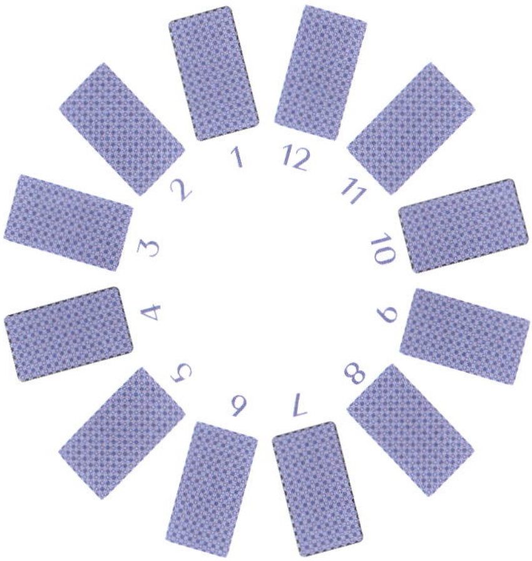

- **Card 1 (first house):** The questioner and their present state
- **Card 2 (second house):** Money and business; material aspects
- **Card 3 (third house):** Relationships with family and friends
- **Card 4 (fourth house):** Family, the house of origin
- **Card 5 (fifth house):** The questioner's loves, affections, children
- **Card 6 (sixth house):** The questioner's profession and state of their health
- **Card 7 (seventh house):** Unions, marriage and associations in general
- **Card 8 (eighth house):** Changes, fatalities, crises
- **Card 9 (ninth house):** Studies, philosophy of life, long journeys
- **Card 10 (tenth house):** Success, affirmation
- **Card 11 (eleventh house):** Friendships, hopes, plans for the future
- **Card 12 (twelfth house):** Inner conflicts, traumas and enemies

MEDITATING WITH THE ARCANA

Now that you're getting used to some of the many methods and their potential, it seems to us that it is the right time to propose a meditation exercise which shows the power of the Tarot as a tool for introspection. How can the Arcana be used for meditation? Let's see together.

Before starting, a brief recommendation: to do the exercises turn off your phone for half an hour, make sure nobody bothers you, breathe slowly and deeply and try to empty your mind of thoughts; light a white candle if you like.

Once the exercise is over, take the necessary time to regain presence within yourself. If you wish you can write down the suggestions that have come to you through the observation of the Arcana.

OVERVIEW

When you find yourself before a spread, look at the images well and pay attention to possible recurrences of numbers and symbols. For example: in front of you there are Justice, the Eight of Swords and the Sun. In this case there will be a prevalence of the number 8 and the suit of Swords, which could be useful for understanding the message that the Arcana are sending you. If, however, the spread proposes many numerical cards or of the same suit, it may indicate an either excessive or deficient imbalance in the characteristics represented by the prevailing suit.

If the cards are all facedown, we suggest that you flip them all, but there is a risk that the question was asked badly. If, there are many cards that represent, for example, similar hats (the Magician, Strength, the Knight of Wands, etc.) it may be a suggestion to use the power of thoughts and active energy.

We obviously invite you to experiment the different similarities that can come up each time, bearing in mind, as we have said, that the 78 Tarot cards are unique and that all the Arcana speak to one another through constant reference. Happy reading!

AWARENESS EXERCISE

Choose the card you love the most and the one you love the least. Observe it attentively while breathing slowly. When you feel ready, transfer the feelings, sensations and ideas that this observation has generated onto paper. You can even use your imagination by drawing or inventing a story. What matters is that you let yourself feel freely. This exercise helps you become familiar with what you like and what you don't like, finding contact with your deepest desire. Every card references an inkling, a memory, a significant figure (for example parents, partners, friends), or it's referred to you, to how you feel in a certain situation, to how you would or would not like to be. It could also help you choose what you truly desire, selecting your goals not only on the basis of what is useful but mainly on the basis of what truly reflects who you are.

USING THE TAROT TO TELL YOUR STORY

"I began by trying to line up Tarot cards at random, to see if I could read a story in them; I looked for other combinations of the same cards; I realized the Tarot is a machine for constructing stories."

The writer Italo Calvino (1923–1985) used these words to describe the path that brought him to write the brief novel *The Castle of Crossed Destinies*, where he uses Tarot cards (the Visconti deck and the Marseille deck) to tell a series of allegorical tales. The cards accompany the pages of the book and become the tool with which the various characters tell their stories. Storytelling through the symbolism of the Tarot isn't just an exercise in style, it can also become a true hero's journey where we are the protagonists and the road we travel is our life. We want to end on a consideration we made at the beginning of this book: we are the Fool that must travel the various phases of human existence, up until the final illumination. Thus, bundle over our shoulder and horizon before us, we are ready to face this fantastic and symbolic journey of ours into the world of the Tarot of Marseille.

CONCLUSIONS

A KNOWLEDGE THAT CONTINUES TO EVOLVE

After reading this book, it is evident that Tarot cannot be viewed as a mere parlor game or bait for the gullible; they are friends that ease the process of listening to ourselves and others. In the context of coaching and counseling, for example, the Tarot can be used to help the person that seeks us out with gaining awareness through active imagination and the projection of our limitations and resources. Since their appearance in our culture, the Tarot has become a topic that impassions both scholars and the curious. Our duty as consultants, scholars or professional help is to update this knowledge by passing it down to future generations after having expanded its depth, awareness, and why not, its narrative qualities.

ACKNOWLEDGEMENTS

First of all, thank you to the publishing house Lo Scarabeo, and to Riccardo Minetti in particular, for making our work possible and for supporting it. Thank you to Gero for his precious advice; to our families and to those who encourage us each day to continue listening and sharing knowledge, emotions and experience committedly.

Finally, a heartfelt thank you to the Tarot of Marseille, silent but eloquent companions in this journey.

Anna Maria Morsucci e *Antonella Aloi*

BIOGRAPHIES OF THE AUTHORS

ANNA MARIA MORSUCCI

Anna Maria Morsucci was born August 12, 1967 in Ostra (province of Ancona); she lives and works in Rome. After getting her degree in Classical Literature she teaches briefly before becoming a journalist; this has been her profession for many years. She deals with personal growth and obtained her certification as a coach from the ICF (International Coach Federation) in 2012. She also handles astrology and the study of Tarot for over twenty years and has developed a significant amount of experience on their use as tools of awareness. She holds astrology and Tarot conferences throughout Italy and has been writing for the main magazines in this sector for years. In 2015 she publishes *God is My Adventure* (editors Spaziointeriore). She collaborates with the journalist Claudio Sabelli Fioretti on the satirical book *The Bastard Horoscope 2013* (editors Chiarelettere). She publishes her first astrology manual in 2017 for Lo Scarabeo, *Astrology for All*, dedicated to the analysis and comprehension of the Natal Theme.

ANTONELLA ALOI

Antonella Aloi is a psychologist and a former graduate in Communication Sciences. She is involved in outreach and training on topics related to psychology and the search for meaning in human beings. She leads individual and group sessions focused on the development of creativity and the enhancement of resources. A scholar of symbology from a self-knowledge perspective, she has written with Anna Maria Morsucci *Tarot of Marseille*, published by Lo Scarabeo. She uses art and symbolism as tools to activate the imagination in herself and others.